# KREATURE KOMFORTS

## THE KORN STORY IN WORDS AND PICTURES

### BY MICHAEL SUMSION

ISBN 1 84240 149 1

TEXT BY **MICHAEL SUMSION**
EDITED BY **BILLY DANCER**
ART DIRECTION AND DESIGN BY **A CREATIVE EXPERIENCE, LONDON**

CHROME DREAMS
PO BOX 230
NEW MALDEN
SURREY KT3 6YY
UK

# CONTENTS

INTRODUCTION

# INTRODUCTION

Within the grand scheme of popular music history, many things can have an effect on the way critics and fans perceive a band and its music. For a start, the band or individual in question must have accumulated a consistently interesting, imaginative and distinctive body of work that renders them worthy of a place in the upper echelons of rock and pop. And any act worth their position in the exalted company of the greats is likely to have contributed to the development of their art form and in turn influenced a variety of other performers and writers in their field and often others.

It is also given that the complexion of popular music has been altered - even if only in some marginal way - by the existence of the artist. This might be a radical and far-reaching change on the cataclysmic level of, say, The Beatles, or could be a no less significant shake-up of a previously moribund genre or style within rock and pop.

The phenomenon known as Korn belong firmly in the latter camp, but their impact on a wider scale is not to be underestimated. Although their music is steeped in the hard rock/heavy metal category, their brazen, catholic mixing of different musical textures and influences has not only won them admiration from within that scene but also plaudits from all other corners of the alternative nation. Indie kids, hip-hop freaks, grunge fanatics and rockers have been quick to praise Korn's irrepressible ecleticism and their injection of buoyancy into a previously jaded hard-rock beast.

Korn are a collective of free-thinking individuals coming at you like a rusty helicopter crash. There is no smug, po-faced artifice to what they do. Actively seeking to challenge themselves and society through intense, provocative and soul-bearing music, their unflinching desire to probe and eradicate mediocrity has been expressed in the form of incendiary assaults on the conventions of rock.

By seamlessly incorporating new influences and styles and putting their own spin on them, Korn have invigorated metal and turned its listeners and bands on to whole new worlds of musical possibilities: grunge, punk, funk and hip-hop are now accepted as part of the scene's musical vocabulary. Before Korn, musical categories were stiff, regimented and disparate entities, with no or little leeway between. Certainly, the notion of absorbing sources as alien to each other as heavy metal, punk and hip-hop was entertained with suspicion until Korn began to merge the boundaries.

Korn frontman Jonathan Davis pens exquisite angst-ridden lyrics based upon his adolescent experiences. His material acts as some kind of emotional catharsis, so that his innermost feelings of alienation and despair do not get buried within his psyche, where they fester. If it wasn't for writing, recording and performing, then there is no knowing what Jonathan would have to do in order to release these feelings and memories.

By his own admission a loner at school, Davis belongs firmly in the classic tradition of singer-songwriters who have transcended pain, insecurity and suicidal tendencies through the medium of music and creativity. The irony is that the art of such brilliant loners encourages an army of virtual 'friends', people who feel they know the artists intimately through their work.

Taut, desperate, furious and militantly creative, Korn deftly wield the urgency of hip-hop, the nihilism of grunge, the celebration of funk and the aggression of punk to the standard hard-rock form and give it a good pasting. Korn make you feel beautifully reckless - every syllable, guitar line and serrated rhythm is invested with complete conviction and adrenaline.

Let us see just how they have come to assume the mantle of most influential and innovative band of the past decade and brushed aside all the second-rate copyists and pretenders in their wake.

# THE REBIRTH

OF ROCK

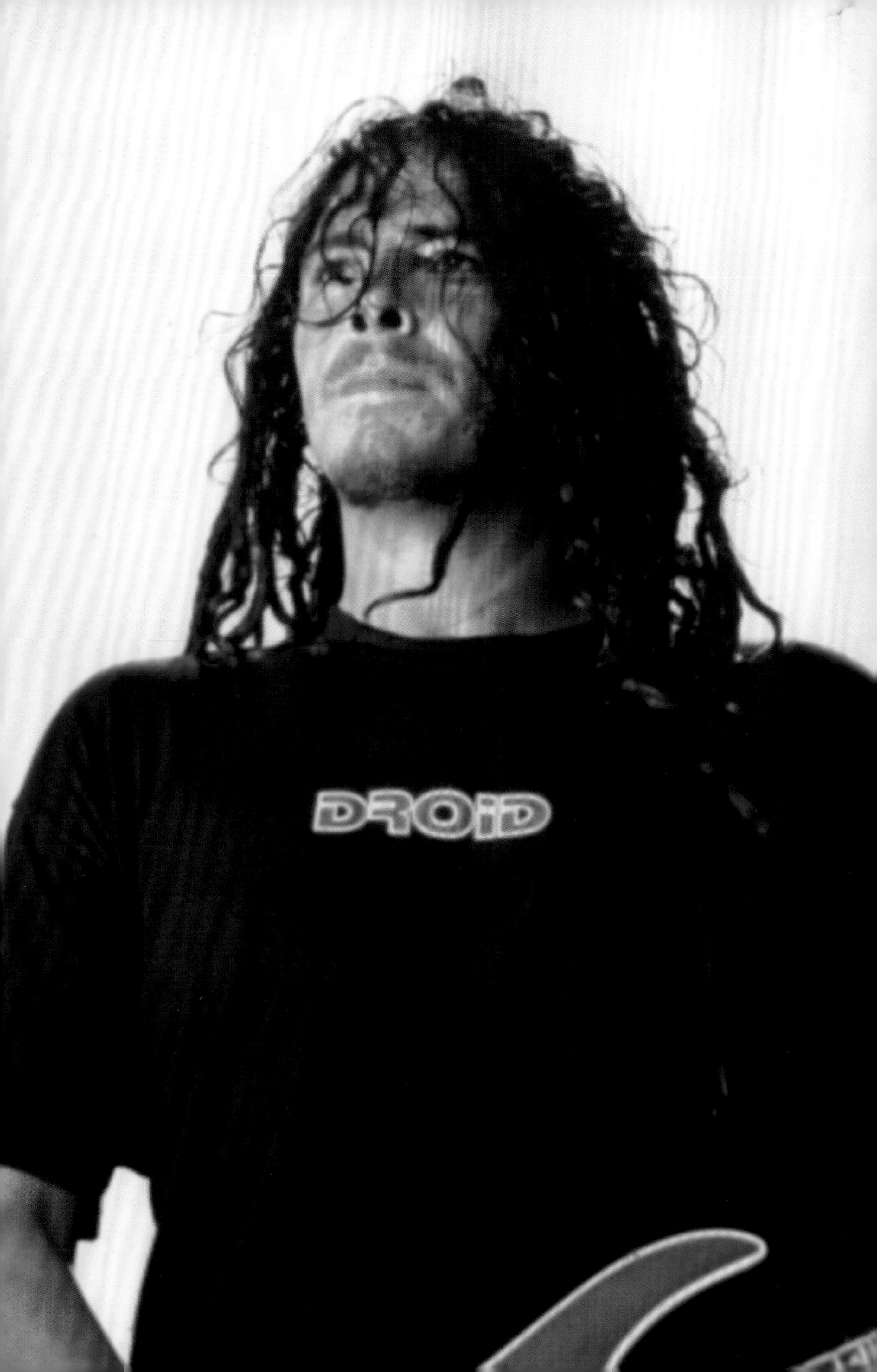
DROID

# THE REBIRTH OF ROCK

The punk revolution of the mid-to-late 1970's was never as integrated into the mainstream in the United States as it was in Britain. The only New Wave bands to have major commercial success, such as Blondie, were forced to file off most of their rough edges to gain acceptance in the mass media. While the likes of the Sex Pistols and the Jam were racking up Top Ten hits and *Top Of The Pops* appearances in their homeland, they remained cult successes in the Land Of The Free, played endlessly on college radio stations, but doomed to late night slots on the more 'respectable media'.

This state of play continued in the 1980's: in the UK, The Smiths and New Order rubbed shoulders with the likes of Wham! but their Stateside equivalents, such as Hüsker Dü and the Pixies, couldn't get arrested. And then, from the unlikely surroundings of the north-western city of Seattle, came the yowling, doomed voice of Kurt Cobain. Nirvana's album *Nevermind*, containing the grunge anthem 'Smells Like Teen Spirit' came out on a major label, Geffen, and suddenly proved that painful realism and commercial success could co-exist. Sadly, the combination proved too much for Cobain, who shot himself in April 1994, but the template was there for other acts to follow.

During the early to mid-1990's the American alternative music scene was in a peculiar state of flux, with many people waiting for something new to explode out of the water and get music lovers enthusiastic again. Grunge had taken a stranglehold over rock, with Nirvana's success spearheading a seemingly endless supply of imitators and bandwagon-jumpers. It hadn't taken long for grunge to descend into a vacuum of hollow Generation X clichés, insipid mediocrity, shameless careerism and creative stasis.

As US rock lost its way amidst the torrent of anodyne, derivative grunge-by-numbers merchants clogging up college radio charts, dormitories and MTV, there seemed little hope for anything life-enhancing, radical and different. With the advent of brit-pop across the Atlantic, alternative music listeners were increasingly cocking their ears to the sounds of Europe and Britain in particular. The cocksure, gun-toting mentality of gangsta-rap held sway amongst many disaffected kids, but for anyone in search of salvation through guitars the situation was bleak.

As for metal, that traditional refuge of the disenfranchised and misunderstood, things looked just as bad. With the music becoming increasingly absurd, bloated and Spinal Tap-esque, even its dedicated followers were beginning to question its relevance.

It had always had its fair share of bombastic cliche and cartoon characters, but the whole scene seemed in danger of collapsing under its own mediocrity and self-importance. Metal had staggered into a laughable state of artistic paralysis and self-parody and grunge had outstayed its welcome as a musical and cultural force. Those acts not trading on their past or churning out tired repetitions of a formula were content to use the metal stereotype and ham it up with a wink to the critics. The very word 'metal' had become a by-word for the worst excesses of masculinity and stunted emotional growth.

The established titans of metal – Black Sabbath, Metallica, Slayer – continued to draw audiences through the festival circuit, and grunge had left an indelible mark on a generation of adolescents and young adults, but there was a discernible thirst for something different to come along and reinvent rock'n'roll. Perhaps it didn't need the impact and all-encompassing sweep of a major youthquake like punk or grunge, just a fresh spin or a new approach.

The rebirth of hard rock as a vibrant art form coincided with two significant developments, namely the shift in public taste and the formation of a red-hot quintet from California known as Korn. As the 90's musical climate made a virtue of cross-pollination and diversity, musicians and listeners alike became drawn to hybrid styles as a route out of rock's creative cul-de-sac. Run-D.M.C. and the Beastie Boys had shown that hip-hop rhythms and mangled guitars could make a potent brew back in the mid-80's, but the trail seemed to run cold there, and 'Walk This Way' now had the unmistakable feel of a novelty hit. The likes of Red Hot Chili Peppers and Jane's Addiction had dabbled with thrashy punk-rock/funk crossover sounds to varying degrees of critical and commercial success, but neither had followed it through. Korn would become the first to defy convention and shake up the scene.

From the debris of two Californian thrashy punk bands, LAPD and Sexart, Korn emerged ready to conquer the world of rock. Setting themselves in opposition to the sterility of metal, ubiquity of grunge and inanity of mainstream chart rock and pop, Korn developed their unique sound by pooling together reference points from all over the musical map.

Building up a steady fan base over a period of years before hitting pay-dirt, Korn stood out from the beginning as a group committed to changing the face of their genre, even inventing a new one along the way. Overlords of pimply-faced, angst-ridden teenagers everywhere, they came to dominate the heavy music scene in America and rule its underworld. Their contemporaries and young upstarts look to them for inspiration and clues as to where music will head.

Always seeking to push back the boundaries of music and add new influences to the melting pot, Korn have achieved the status of leaders of the hard-rock fraternity by aping the ethics of the punk rockers of the 1970's and the hip-hop stars of the 1980's. They have looked into the eyes and souls of their core audience and served back their dreams, frustrations, anxieties and aspirations writ large. This remarkable group offer a ready-made soundtrack to their lives, a vehicle for their fears, a temporary antidote to the drudgery of everyday life. In a word, consolation.

From the start, Korn always made great claims about their music. All five members share the belief that nobody can match the level of commitment to be found within the group. Both the band's claims to greatness and their collective decision-making have evolved to fruition with perfect symmetry. This has bolstered their unity and imposed an almost overbearing fear of breaking the chain. So, as the individual trust strengthens, the group's reputation as single-minded artists intensifies. Nothing can disrupt the ascent of Korn.

Conceived as a reaction to the pseudo-angst of middle-class bands like Rage Against The Machine, the cynicism of corporate grunge and the tired cabaret of Motley Crue and the like, Korn went out on a limb from the beginning and pursued their own vision. No bullshit, just honesty and integrity. Other groups might have paid lip-service to trends or the limited expectations of fans and the industry, but this is one that wanted to explore all possibilities. In doing so, they have produced some of the most enduring music of the 1990's.

Theirs is a body of work that grows more influential by the day and impresses by its sheer quality. It would be naive to overestimate the cultural importance of the group, but there is no doubting their cult credibility. They might not yet have enjoyed the mammoth mainstream success as their historical counterparts, but there is the same discernible valour, adventure and timeless quality about their work that is certain to ensure its longevity. Korn are unafraid to take risks, push forward boundaries, deploy a whole host of musical styles and bring them all together under one distinct umbrella. Their music veers all over the place and on first listen sounds disjointed and schizophrenic. However, as their multitudes of fans and the countless bands they've influenced will attest, it makes sense and is forthright and honest.

2000 was the year in which metal/hip-hop crossover went mainstream and mega, not just in the US but all over Europe as well. The seeds sown by Korn blossomed to great effect, influencing groups of the calibre of Limp Bizkit, At The Drive-In, Amen, ...And You Will Know Us By The Trail Of Dead, Papa Roach and Queens Of The Stone Age, all of whom capitalised on a new found acceptance of all things hard, heavy, brattish, angsty and sincere. Producer Ross Robinson, who helped shape the sound and career of Korn, was in the midst of it all, the lynchpin linking stadium rock with the underground.

Ironically, many of the fans of this new movement will have come flocking to the stadiums and record shops blissfully unaware that it all started way earlier with Jonathan Davis and his cohorts. This popular explosion owes a great debt to the pioneering work done by Korn in rock's underground in the 1990's, a scene that sprung up organically without MTV exposure or double-page pull-outs in magazines.

At the pinnacle stood five brave, earnest, inspired, creative talents united in a desire to lay down the heaviest, most intense and original rock'n'roll since the days of The Sex Pistols, MC5 and The Stooges. Utilising the same basic tools associated with a rock band, but experimenting with a wider sonic palette, Korn intended to deliver a brand new direction to this music and pulled it off with aplomb. Universally admired amongst the new breed of producers, artists and writers, they have stood out from the pack from their earliest days - and still do.

# CHAPTER 2

BORN IN

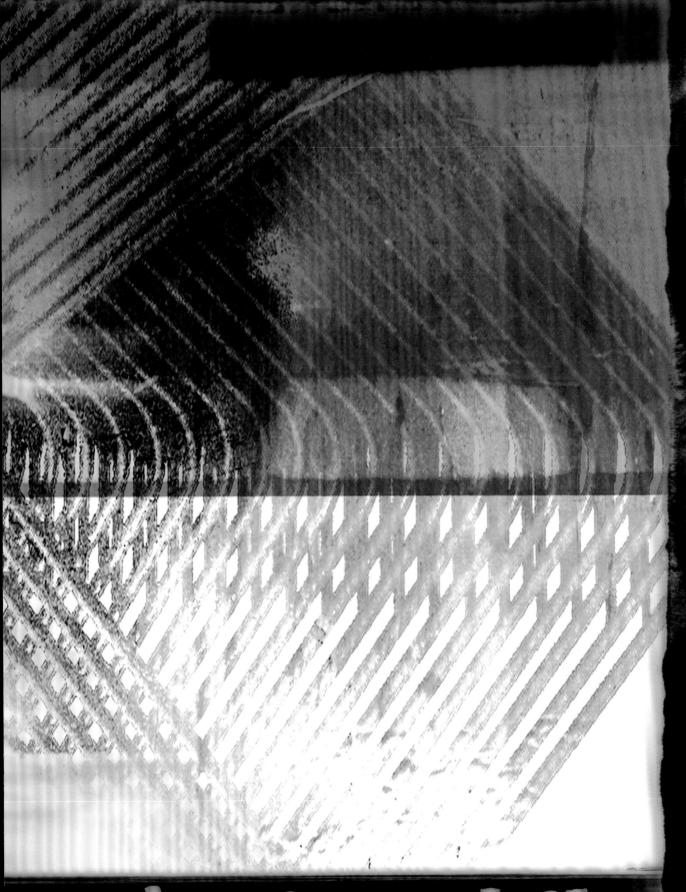

BAKERSFIELD

# BORN IN BAKERSFIELD

On 18th January 1971, Jonathan Houseman Davis made his entry to the world. Born of Scottish parents, he grew up in Bakersfield, California, where he attended Highland High School. Jonathan's mother was an actress and dancer in local theatrical productions, while his father, Rick Davis, played keyboards for country music pioneer Buck Owens, among others. He also ran a musical store and managed Owens' recording studio in Bakersfield.

But the young Jonathan's childhood was far from easy. His early years left scars that have taken years to heal, deeply affecting his outlook and musical creativity. For when he was just three years old, his parents divorced under the messiest of circumstances. His father later remarried when Jonathan was 12. While divorce is now a fact of life in the Western world, and children's reactions to it differ enormously, it was obvious that his parents' split hit Jonathan deeper than most.

As a child, Jonathan grew increasingly resentful of his dad and accused him of screwing up his upbringing by leaving home. Rick Davis was often on the road in bands and busy with his work, leaving his mother to cope with bringing up the children alone. In Jonathan's eyes, he conformed to the classic stereotype of absent father, neglecting his offspring and acting in a selfish and insensitive way. Needless to say, this behaviour left an indelible imprint upon his young sons' consciousness. Jonathan grew increasingly angry and felt that his father was mistreating his whole family. Their relationship wasn't the warmest, with very little emotional contact. On the rare occasions when Rick was around, their conversations amounted to little more than crude discussions about the opposite sex. In fact, this remained the case until Jonathan began writing songs that addressed his feelings for his father.

Rick Davis played in bands with Korn bassist Fieldy's father for many years. Having this raucous pair as role models influenced their own debauchery in the early days, but in turn served as a warning in later life. When his own baby boy Nathan was born, Jonathan realised from bitter experience that he had to sharpen up his act.

Most disturbing, traumatic and psychologically significant of all was the sexual abuse perpetrated by a family friend on the young Jonathan. He summoned up the courage to tell his parents about what happened, but they refused to believe it and thought it was a figment of their child's overactive imagination. The non-reaction of his parents was as devastating and hurtful as the abuse itself. This

Jonathan's first musical stirrings developed whilst messing around in his father's Bakersfield music store. By the age of just five, he had taken up drumming. He began picking up other instruments in the store and getting noises out of them. The ever keen and resourceful Jonathan asked the music teachers giving lessons in the store if they could tutor him in the basics of each instrument. Once he'd grasped them, he was off and running, teaching himself the rest.

By the time he reached high school, Jonathan had mastered a range of instruments, including piano and the bagpipes, and won medals at various Scottish games. His grandmother had played the pipes, and Jonathan was moved to take them up after hearing a rendition of the evergreen 'Amazing Grace'. He performed in his high school band as well as in a bagpipe group.

The music-hungry Jonathan was obsessed with making it, but his father was only too familiar with the notoriously fickle, ruthless and ultra-competitive music business and warned him away from it. Time after time, Jonathan's requests for assistance faced firm refusals from Rick, whose experiences had coloured his perspective. Once again he wasn't there to help when Jonathan needed him most. This increased the level of tension and antagonism between father and son, but in the long term strengthened Jonathan's resolve and desire to succeed on his own terms.

As he grew up, Jonathan became more and more immersed in music, whether it be playing or listening, adding double-bass, violin and clarinet to his accomplishments. But this gawky misfit was often tormented by fellow students, who viewed him as 'different' and 'alien'. His difficulties as an unpopular youth were drawn upon heavily as subject matter in his later role as songwriting genius for Korn.

In his ultra-conformist high school, he was bullied by the jocks in the football team. Freaked out by his decision to wear eyeliner and his love of Duran Duran, they hurled homophobic abuse at him throughout school. He was called 'gay', 'queer' and 'faggot' (hence the Korn song 'Faget') by narrow-minded classmates who didn't want to understand. This put a lot of pressure on Jonathan and made him feel lonely and isolated. Even at this young age he'd experienced enough hurt, pain, anguish and mental torture to last a lifetime, but he hung in there and developed a defence strategy.

If these morons were going to call him gay and say he had AIDS, he was going to throw that back in their faces. This was the origin of Jonathan's controversial 'HIV' tattoo. It would become a life-saver for him, as there were occasions when lust and passion took precedence over the brain. The tattoo served as a chilling reminder that anybody he had sex with could theoretically be infected with the virus. Jonathan even went so far to claim that the tattoo should be compulsory, as there are too many people with HIV having unsafe sex and disregarding the consequences of their actions.

Over the years, Jonathan attracted much criticism for his tattoo, mainly from people who saw it as a cruel, sick joke or evidence of a perceived hostility towards homosexuals. A journalist from *Interview* magazine found it particularly offensive and told Jonathan so, but the Korn leader put him straight in no uncertain terms. Jonathan has gone on record as stating that he is neither homosexual nor homophobic, and neither is he HIV-positive.

On his right arm, in contrast, Jonathan has a tattoo of a bishop ripping through his skin, supposedly a metaphor for the atrocities carried out in the name of institutionalised religion. Born a Catholic, this disdain for religion and dogma marked him out as different and eccentric, but he had seen through the lies of the church at an early age. Despite being the butt of many people's ridicule at school and in his home environment, Jonathan assumed the

role of an outsider looking in at a sick, bigoted society. He refused to bow down to other people's expectations, values and ideas, and developed a strong sense of individuality. He loathed the sheep-like mentality of the crowd and would not change or adapt his views and outlook on life to accommodate other people, believing that you should always be true to yourself. This admirable philosophy manifested itself from the earliest days in Korn material such as 'Lies' and 'Fake', both vivid songs that deal with the insincerity, hypocrisy and conformity that can often be found in society. Their author had realised at a young age that people are too scared to be themselves and prefer to follow the mainstream.

After graduating from high school, Jonathan studied for two semesters and secured a job at the coroner's office in Kern County. His initial motives were a desperate, morbid fascination with the dead and a desire to witness a real dead body in the flesh. Expecting it to be an interesting experience, he slowly grew to love the job and became absorbed in the profession, eventually becoming a reserve deputy coroner. This involved going to the scenes of accidents, checking the fatalities and writing up reports.

Continuing until he joined Korn at the age of 22, Davis witnessed the gruelling results of murders, suicides and car accidents. This instilled in him a fear of cars that persists to this day, and he barely ever drives. Though he initially recoiled at the prospect of having to apply a scalpel to a corpse, he soon developed an obsession with the work, loving its adrenaline rush and what he considered to be a power trip. He thrived on the challenge of trying to work out the circumstances surrounding each death. Jonathan described his time spent at the coroners as "death, death, crying and grief". Some of the shocking images still resonate and linger to this day. He even had to inspect the bodies of people he knew.

One of the corpses was that of a young victim of incest. Though at first, he managed to keep focused, professional and detached, this body started to haunt him so much that his dreams revolved around her. After a while, dreams about the dead he'd seen began to consume him and led to him suffering from Post-Traumatic Stress Disorder. These experiences hardened Jonathan and made him realise that life rarely turns out as one imagines. He learned that by the nature of their job, coroners become cold and matter-of-fact about death.

But Jonathan wasn't the only dysfunctional musical adolescent in the area. Reginald 'Fieldy' Arvizu came into the world on the 2nd of November 1969, while his parents were on tour with his fathers band. The tour bus pulled over from the main road and Fieldy's mother gave birth to a bass legend in the making. As well as playing with Jonathan's father, Fieldy's dad also used to be in a band with Brian 'Head' Welch's musically minded parent.

Heralded as a unique, powerhouse bass player, Fieldy started early, getting his hands on his first bass guitar at the age of 5. His nickname derived from his fat chipmunk cheeks as a child. His friends started calling him Gopher, which got abbreviated to Garr. In turn, this became Garfield, then Fieldy and Fieldy Snuts ('Feel These Nuts'). Everybody eventually settled on Fieldy (phew!) and the name has stuck ever since.

West Coast hip-hop played a pivotal role in his musical education, and he learned to play by picking out the sinewy bass lines from dusty old funk and early hip-hop and rap records. He soon developed the percussive bottom-end sound that would become so distinctive. When he began playing, he stumbled upon the Ibanez Sound Gear series of bass guitars. They initially appealed because they were smaller than other instruments, but once he actually played one he was in heaven. The sound he got out of it seemed better and clearer than all the others.

As a teenager, Fieldy had a stab at playing 6-string guitar through his father's encouragement, but soon gave it up. He grabbed a bass when his friend Head needed a player for his group, a cheesy, clichéd rock band. At first, he didn't contribute very much, but when he realised the potential of his instrument he buckled down and enslaved himself to perfecting his art.

Head, or Brian Phillip Welch as his parents preferred to call him, was born on the 19th of June 1970 in Torrance, California. Unlike Fieldy's convoluted label, the source of Head's nickname was quite straightforward - he can't get a hat to fit! Another early starter, he began playing guitar at the age of 10 and struck up a friendship with James 'Munky' Shaffer through high school. Before there was even a thought of Korn in anyone's mind, he was hanging out with Munky, teaching each other guitar parts to songs. Their competitive but healthy relationship spurred each other on to become as good as they could be and conspired to create the most admired dual guitar attack in modern rock.

Realising during adolescence that rock'n'roll was his destiny and that it was a hard taskmaster, he dedicated himself to the guitar and procured a dazzling reputation by the time he came to join Korn. Rated as a "really bad guitar player" by his bandmates, he is also recognised as the most naturally gifted member.

His partner in fret-crime, James Christian 'Munky' Shaffer was born in Rosedale, California, on the 6th of June 1970. His nickname, like Head's, derived from an anatomical anomaly: when he shared a two-bedroom apartment with Fieldy and five others, Fieldy christened him 'Munky' after noticing his bare feet, which apparently resemble monkey-hands when spread out.

In a roundabout way, a glittering career in rock'n'roll stemmed from Munky sneaking out of the house one night to catch a party in the neighbourhood. Pushing his bike, the chain slipped off, so he slapped his hand on it so it wouldn't make a noise. However, his finger got caught on the chain and cut the top off. The guitar maestro started playing his instrument as part of the therapy for his mutilated digit. He began learning on a guitar that had been packed away in his closet at home, and never looked back.

Munky has always maintained, though, that he wouldn't have got started in music if it hadn't been for his best friend, Brian 'Head' Welch, who inspired and encouraged him from the beginning. Even Head's parents did their bit, allowing Munky to raid their fridge and eat with them so he could save his lunch money to buy a guitar amplifier.

Munky and Fieldy began playing on the Bakersfield rock scene, initially under the name LAPD (the standard abbreviation for the Los Angeles Police Department, but in this instance 'Love And Peace, Dude', or, later, 'Laughing As People Die'). One day Fieldy's answering machine picked up the message "Do you guys need a drummer?" And another piece of the jigsaw fell into place.

David Randall Silveria was born on September 21, 1972 in Bakersfield. By his own admission, he started learning to play the drums mainly because there was very little else to occupy a young child in that dead-end town. Beginning at the age of 9, David evolved his personal style through constant practice and a desire to improve all the time. He didn't obtain his own drum kit until he was 13, and never took any formal lessons or used a tuition book. The only drawback for his new LAPD bandmates was that he was still at school and his mother had to drive him to band practice because he was so young.

So far, so conventional. Four talented musicians, in a town that didn't appreciate them. But the catalyst that would set them on the road to world domination had yet to be added to the volatile mix.

CHAPTER3

ON THE ROAD

TO IMMORTALITY

# ON THE ROAD TO IMMORTALITY

Although all five members of Korn were raised in Bakersfield, they prefer to say they're from Orange County. This is because of the bands somewhat ambivalent attitude towards their home town, which they have gone on record as denouncing for being full of 'white trash' and 'hicks' who like nothing better than a public brawl.

Jonathan particularly came to hate Bakersfield with a passion as he grew up, and has described it as "evil". Like many small towns, there was nothing to occupy young kids outside of school, so the obvious avenues to explore were fighting, drug taking or music. Although Jonathan got involved in the first two, fortunately he chose to pursue the last as a career.

While he was working in the coroner's office, he fronted an act called Sexart, who, at the time, were just one more bunch of rockers in a nondescript town just a little too far from LA to be noticed. In retrospect, there was a lot of talent kicking around in the band's ranks: not only would their frontman go on to be one of the most respected vocalists in rock, but future members of Orgy, Videodrone, Cradle Of Thorns and Juice were playing behind him at various times. At their sporadic gigs, Sexart would also perform a certain number called 'Blind', that would eventually become known way beyond the hick towns of Southern California.

Meanwhile, LAPD had relocated to LA. The line-up at this stage comprised Fieldy on bass, Munky on guitar, David on drums and singer Richard Morales, with the ever-loyal Head a permanent fixture in a non-playing capacity. They were learning their licks on the pay-to-play circuit, handing over their money to promoters and venue owners in the hope of getting some attention from the music industry. It certainly seemed to get them somewhere, as they cut an EP, *Love And Peace, Dude*, which in turn led to a contract with the prestigious Triple X label (home to Jane's Addiction) and a full-length album, *Who's Laughing Now*.

Unfortunately, success seemed to be too much for certain egos in the band, and LAPD split up in 1991. However, they regrouped shortly afterwards, this time without Morales, but with occasional guitar duties performed by Head. They also underwent a name-change, calling themselves Creep.

Ironically, considering they'd made the pilgrimage to Los Angeles, it was a brief return trip to Bakersfield, in 1993, that took them to superstar status. Munky and Head were in a bar when they heard a striking voice. Up to that point they'd barely noticed the band on stage - who were, of course, Sexart.

Within a week, Munky and Head were on the telephone to Jonathan, inviting him to join their band. Initially, Jonathan wasn't keen - it would mean ditching his pals in Sexart and giving up his day job at the coroner's office. But a meeting with an astrologer persuaded him to seize the chance and jam with Creep at their base in Orange County. After three songs, he was in.

Enticed by the prospect of moving to LA, Jonathan accepted the offer and wasted no time in stamping his own imprint on the group. To symbolise a clean break with the past, the five brainstormed some ideas for a new band name, and came up with Korn. There have been numerous explanations for this decision, the most disturbing being that it's a contraction of 'Child Pornography', but the most succinct view came from David. "It kind of means that it doesn't matter what your band's called," said the drummer. "...because, 'Korn', that's a dumb name, but once a band gets established, that makes a name cool."

The second major difference that Jonathan made to the group was his conscious decision to give them a fresh musical direction. To his ears, Creep were slightly too upbeat and effervescent for a ballsy rock band, and he wanted to steer them into darker territory, as much lyrically as musically. With the settled line-up in place, and now firmly ensconced in the Southern California rock scene, Korn threw themselves into the music, jamming round the block, writing and recording material and honing their live show. These early days on the road were far from idyllic, touring in an R.V. with a trailer attached to it. On the very first day, the trailer, which carried instruments, amps and drums, broke down no fewer than four times.

One of their most memorable early gigs, their fourth, was at a packed club in Santa Monica Boulevard, where a member of the audience threw stink-bombs all over the venue, thereby emptying the place within minutes. However the band were so focused and centred on their music that they played on, oblivious to the smell. Korn had also suffered having beer thrown in their face at gigs, but high spirits turned really nasty one night when Munky had a pocket-knife hurled at him on stage. Luckily, it narrowly missed him, getting stuck in his guitar cabinet.

The band duly hired a manager and recorded a demo tape of material with which to tempt record company A&R representatives. From the start, Korn were determined to get signed, holding no truck with the elitist

snobbery of the alternative rock cognoscente who'd prefer to keep everything under-publicised and underground.

When it came to getting noticed by record companies, the ecleticism of Korn proved something of a stumbling block. Industry chiefs eager to label, package and market their bands as product, scratched their heads in trying to understand their style. Hitting the listener as they did from various corners of the musical vocabulary, Korn lacked a handy peg, a pigeonhole or easily recognisable label with which to slot them into the market place.

Korn would come to be labelled as many things by a media desperate to invent or define new trends in music - be it metal, alternative, hardcore, punk or rap-rock crossover - but nobody, least of all the band itself, seemed able to agree on which category best suited them. Korn's diverse, experimental sound alienated an industry that had grown wearily accustomed to churning out endless slight variations on a similar proven, successful theme. Although they never for one moment contemplated giving up on their dream or abandoning their principles, Korn grew impatient and frustrated with the cynicism and narrow horizons of the conservative music business.

Eventually, Korn's dogged persistence paid off, and labels began pricking up their ears. Heavyweights of the stature of RCA and Atlantic began talking to the band and even offered them contracts on the basis of the demo tape. Admirably however, Korn plumped for the independent label, Immortal, a subdivision of Epic Records, because the company's executives were knocked out by the tape and displayed a genuine enthusiasm for their music. Recording for an indie also ensured more artistic freedom, understanding, empathy and a healthier, more intimate working relationship.

Armed with a small advance from Immortal, Korn set about recording a full-length album at the Indigo Ranch Studios in Malibu, with producer Ross Robinson at the helm. If any one person is responsible for the resurgence of heavy rock music in the 1990's and beyond, it has to be Robinson, whose credits also include Limp Bizkit, Slipknot, Deftones and Amen.

It was at this precise moment that the music world got its wake-up call, for Korn were about to embark on an adventure that would have repercussions for the heavy scene in particular as well as the record industry as a whole. "ARE YOU READY?" bellowed Jonathan. It was effectively a declaration of war.

# CHAPTER 4

A NEW CUTTING EDGE

# A NEW CUTTING EDGE

One of the secrets of Korn's success, apart from their evident talent, is their ability to market themselves and to tap into what the fans want from them. The group promoted the release of *Korn* by handing out flyers at free gigs with the likes of House of Pain and Biohazard. Each flyer included a questionnaire which, when filled in, would reward the punter with a free sampler of the album.

Released in North America on July 7th 1994, Korn's self-titled debut album announced to the world that an inspirational new force had arrived in heavy music. It was crystal clear that this band were breaking new ground and creating a shift in rock in the process - away from the predictable formula sound that had dominated for so long, and towards something as yet undefined but hungry, fresh, vigorous, exciting, exotic and inventive. A feast of hip-hop-tinged rock, grunge-powered metal and woozy funk, the debut was one of the definitive records of its era.

Nobody, least of all the band members themselves, could have foreseen the impact this album would have upon the whole music scene. The cover shows a pretty little blonde-haired girl in a purple dress, sitting on a playground swing as she's menaced by an unseen figure – all that's visible is his ominous shadow. It's like a 1950's 'don't talk to strangers tract' reworked by a Goth with chronic depressive tendencies. The inside sleeve contained pornographic material that would have shocked the parents of many of Korn's target audience.

For their first record the band endeavoured to reproduce their live sound as faithfully as possible, without too much over the top production. Using an old Neve analogue mixing-desk and relatively antiquated equipment was deemed to be necessary in order to get across a warmer, more organic live feel, and the end product more than justifies that decision. Producer Ross Robinson was delighted with the album, and was moved to tell them that one day they'd be selling millions of records. Very much a kindred spirit, Robinson saw things as Korn did and shared a similar approach to making music.

From the head-spinning blast of the show-opening track 'Blind' through to the infamous 'Daddy', the album was a fully-formed, self-contained masterpiece of fearsome vitriol, masterful dynamics and unexpected musical turns. From the adrenaline rush that was 'Ball Tongue' to the irreverent 'Shoots And Ladders', the turbo-charged 'Divine' and multi-layered 'Need To', listeners were bamboozled and transported by the bewildering range of emotions and musicality offered to them. This cross-pollinated sonic assault valued tone and texture over distortion and volume, incorporating industrial-strength guitars, hip-hop, macho posturing, sensitivity, violent fantasy and gruelling realism.

By giving rock a healthy dose of blitzkrieg hip-hop, angry rap and rubbery funk rhythms, set to angst-fuelled lyrics that constituted a primal scream into the abyss, Korn were speaking for a new generation hitherto deprived of an authentic, dissenting voice. For the lyrics of Jonathan Davis were straight from the gut, ringing out across America with sincerity, clarity and great power.

These largely autobiographical tales depicted a lost, fragmented childhood and were delivered with such fierce emotion and energy that they won their author immediate respect and admiration from newly converted fans everywhere. The emotional ties and level of identification between Jonathan and his fans were established and would contribute hugely to Korn's growing popularity. Whereas other bands mostly dealt in fraudulent emotional pornography, Korn delivered authenticity and the pungent smell of truth.

The entire record, in fact, was conceived as a grand metaphor for childhood, almost a lament for the point at which maturity impinges upon innocence. From the picture of a young girl on the cover, to the child's writing on the inside sleeve and the mocking misspelling of their name, the album was soaked in the imagery of childhood. The strange blend of influences theoretically contradicted each other, but, patched together with a magpie zeal and fox-like cunning, gave the songs an atmosphere and quality all of their own. Murderous drum arrangements, spectral riffs, thundering bass and desolate vocals contrived to produce a spectacular noise that oozed energy, terror and catharsis.

The bludgeoning opener 'Blind', an old Sexart song, is a thinly veiled reference to his early drug use, containing the lines: "Another place I find to escape the pain inside... See through the grey that clouds my mind". Here Jonathan was putting himself on the line with an almost naked vulnerability, admitting that drugs once controlled his life and coloured his thought processes. They provided an easy escape from his childhood and temporarily offered solace from his confusion and pain. He wanted to rid his mind of its anguish but wasn't self-assured enough to make it happen. He used drugs as a prop to distort reality and escape from the world.

'Ball Tongue', contrary to popular myth, is not about oral sex but another bleak, autobiographical essay. It's about a T-shirt designer called Jeff Creath, who fell out with the band many moons ago, and hoped to be famous through his brief Korn association: "There you are alone, with no hope of ever having something to be proud of, something earned without begging". Jonathan claims he can't even remember if the 'ball tongue' was a piercing or a wart.

The implication was that Jonathan had trusted him enough to share some of his innermost feelings and secrets. And Creath became obsessed with Jonathan, expecting him to be there all the time: "Yes, I know you're the person, the person that took time with me/Does it give you the right to expect your life revolves around me?" When Jonathan withdrew from their relationship, the T-shirt guy vented some pent-up frustration by double-crossing Jonathan and the band.

Some of Jonathan's most chilling lines feature in 'Ball Tongue', none more so than the candid and vitriolic: "Why are you at home buried in your own self-pity?/Why do you insist on living the life clean out of me?" Set in the doomed romantic's milieu of late-night rainy streets, shadowy bars and shabby bed-sits, they relate the bruised life of the emotional outsider, trampled by his acutely painful memories but never quite ready to surrender.

Lines such as these utterly transcended the conservatism of hard rock and introduced the genre to a whole new lexicon, with their haunting, stark, terse poetry stripped down to bare bones. These were songs of life on the edge between hope and defeat, redemption and despair.

'Need To' expands upon the theme of fear of rejection, of being in a relationship with somebody whom you find impossible to trust completely. The song details Jonathan's fear of getting too close to somebody in case they stop loving him and walk away. Caught up in a cycle of mistrust and pessimism, Jonathan had become accustomed to betrayal in relationships and had developed a misanthropy that was preventing him from moving on and opening up to life again: "You pull me closer, I push you away/You tell me it's OK, I can't help but feel the pain". Addressing the girl in the song with "I hate you...Fuck you, bitch", it was evident that he'd decided to resent her before the relationship got off the ground purely because he was certain that she'd end up leaving him. The language here demonstrates why Korn's lyrics are sometimes criticised for apparent misogyny – although in the depths of pain like this, one can understand that politically correct language isn't the top priority.

'Clown' tells a tale from the band's early days, when a skinhead spectator took a swing at Jonathan during a concert in San Diego. There's an ambiguous note of pity towards the assailant: "A tattooed body to hide who you are/Scared to be honest, be yourself", speaks for those who don't have the courage to rise above the herd. The tale also confirms that, although he's now a rock star, Jonathan still feels like the runty weirdo in junior high, getting picked on by the jocks. Despite the bravado in the lyrics ("Clown you ain't shit, turn round and get your face split") it should be remembered that it was Korn's manager who ended up flattening the skinhead.

'Divine' is a revenge fantasy based upon another rejection. The tables turn when an ex-lover returns to Jonathan and expresses a desire to give it another go. "You're suffering 'cause of me, it's divine" and "Did you really think you'd beat me at my own game?" are lines that encapsulate the writer's bitterness at the time, as well as expressing a new-found sense of power over that person. He obviously wished to show how it felt to long for somebody you couldn't have, and to emphasise that he wasn't a doll who could be picked up and thrown away at her whim. He perfectly captures the ambivalent emotions of such tactics with the lines: "You know what, fuck you/I'm fed up with you/I'm not as good as you/Fuck, no, I'm better than you". But there's a distinct air that Jonathan doesn't really believe himself, that he's still trapped in a pit of self-loathing and low self-esteem.

'Faget' attracted much controversy from critics who surmised that it was an attack on the homosexual community. Actually, it was a raw, dramatic outpouring of angst from his teenage years. It was an exorcism of despair from being subjected to a torrent of homophobic abuse from high school jocks, who thought nothing of calling him 'pussy', 'queer' and 'faggot'. The track reflected on a period in which a New Romantic, Duran Duran-worshipping Jonathan donned make-up and hung out in gay bars. He has always denied that he ever went through a homosexual stage. Having been the recipient of homophobia all his life, he decided that he couldn't fight it so claims he made a joke of it. The line "you can suck my dick and fuckin' like it!" may have been a joke too far, however...

'Shoots And Ladders' deals with the often-unpleasant stories behind seemingly innocent children's nursery rhymes. Children shouldn't be given sanitised nuggets of reality, devoid of context: 'London Bridge Is Falling Down' is really about the Great Fire Of London and 'Ring o' Roses' is about the bubonic plague, and kids should know this. "Look at the pages that caused this evil" declaims Jonathan, as if 'Nick Nack Paddywack' was the source of all the troubles of the world. The weird thing is, so committed is his performance, you almost believe it could be.

'Predictable' returns to the inevitability of getting hurt in a relationship. Within this song, Jonathan actually went as far as to say that he'd rather die than endure the pain of rejection. He claims that "I can in every way, mistake the pain I feel inside/It comes to me, evil thoughts just creeping through my mind". Every day brings a choice between "I'm gonna try" and "I'm gonna die": the effort of existence when there doesn't seem to be a point and the release of suicide.

'Fake' examines the insincerity of people who hide behind an image of what they think others want them to be. People are so scared of being seen to be different that they will change their opinions and appearance to fit in with the crowd, the mainstream: "I can't stand the sight of you/I can't stand what you put me through/Your life's a lie, that you hide/Is it that terrible being you inside?" Yet again, we're back in high school with Jonathan, the eternal outsider, who dared to listen to Duran Duran while everyone else was raising their lighters to Heart and Foreigner. But, for all the pain, he knows which side he'd rather be on.

The more affirmative lines, " You try so hard to be wanted/False emotions tells you fronted/I think being a person relies on one thing/Be yourself, let you come through", could be read as Jonathan's philosophy of life. He warns his former tormentors that they will realise they've wasted their lives at school by trying to fit in with the accepted trend or view-point: "Fake, you'll regret it, you'll regret it!"

'Lies' is another variation on the theme, containing the immortal words "I want you to see the life you have disguised". He points the finger at his persecutors: "Do you ever see from outside your fears?" And the aggression that's been seething inside him for so many years erupts in the grisly image "My life is ripping your heart out and destroying my pain." It's like something out of Stephen King's *Carrie*, as the eternal victim has her gore-splattered revenge on the beautiful people who are ugly as sin inside.

From grotesque punishment fantasies to embarrassing medical problems. The penultimate cut, 'Helmet In The Bush', is an account of Jonathan's penis retraction, a condition caused by persistent amphetamine abuse. The line, "Please God let me sleep tonight", refers to the resulting insomnia. "Don't hit my stick"... well, we can leave that to your imagination, can't we? Unpleasant as the symptoms are, it's impossible not to smile as Jonathan pleads "Please God save me/From my painful situation," for all the world as if he's a desperate patient in a *Carry On* movie.

'Daddy', the haunting, hushed, painstakingly slow album closer, featuring the harrowing cries of the lead singer, is the track that takes *Korn* to another dimension. Although many leapt on the sensitive, inflammatory material, surmising that the abuser in the song was Jonathan's father, his assailant was a family friend. He had gone to his father for help but wasn't taken seriously. The song was conceived as a plea for his father to understand his pain and anguish. In a way, the song ties together all the elements of the whole album, from the nursery rhyme imagery to the disturbing cover. "A rape in mind and on your flesh I'll eat" is a combination of the homicidal paedophiles that haunt modern society with their mythical, historical antecedents, the ghouls and trolls and bogeymen who will eat up children if they don't eat their greens or say their prayers.

Jonathan's desperate, battle-scarred howls, sobs and screams - "I fucking hate you!/You fucking ruined my life!" - are an acquired taste but are guaranteed to make the hairs on the listener's neck stand on end. But that's not all - there's a bizarre 'hidden' track some 14 minutes after the album proper had finished, consisting of a recording of a vicious row between a husband and wife over a car repair manual. Its origins are a complete mystery to everyone connected with the recording - it was on a tape that Ross Robinson acquired years before when he was cleaning an apartment. Is the marital mudslinging meant to throw 'Daddy' into sharp relief, contrasting real agony with banal domestic discomfort? Or does it say that pain can fester even in the most ideal circumstances? Incidentally, diehard fans claim you can hear the man fart at one point in the recording.

This monumental, sprawling opus was warmly received by critics and fans alike, and quickly went double platinum in the USA as well as racking up phenomenal sales in Canada, New Zealand and Australia. It also scored the group a Grammy award nomination for Best Metal Performance Of The Year. *Metal Hammer* magazine compared the arrival of Korn to the reformation of The Beatles even before the album was released, praising its relentless consistency and visceral energy.

A close, intense bond between the battle-scarred Jonathan Davis and his growing ranks of fans was developing, and Korn were determined not to let this early success change them or go to their heads. They were adamant that they weren't about to turn into sad, distant, clichéd rock stars, well aware that without the fans they were nothing.

Korn's method in crossing over would be a far cry from the time-honoured one of mass commercial saturation, high-rotation radio and MTV exposure. Without expensive publicity, video posturing or the hyperbole of publicity, they made their way through the rock firmament by tireless touring, grass-roots support and local self-promotion.

Immediately after the album's release, Korn set about spreading the word as far as they could. Constant jamming together, intense rehearsals and the adrenaline flow of the live gigs enabled the quintet to cultivate a fluency lacking in LAPD, Creep and Sexart. Korn were received particularly well in Europe, where the band were knocked out by the fervent response of their audiences (and the quality of pornography in Amsterdam).

At the same time as he was being propelled into the role of spokesman for a generation that couldn't cope with conventional society, Jonathan was coming to terms with an utterly conventional aspect of reality – he was about to become a father. His girlfriend Renée, who had been with him throughout his time with Korn, gave birth to Nathan Houseman Davis on October 18th, 1995. It was a lucky escape for the new arrival – had Renée produced a girl, as Jonathan was convinced she would, he wanted to call her Salaam Dementia. Parenthood moderated his excesses, but these things are relative – on his first concert after Nathan's birth, Jonathan got through fifteen shots of Jack Daniel's.

Korn's individual, unclassifiable style endeared them to fans of all styles of music – they were as likely to land support slots with hip-hop acts like House of Pain or Cypress Hill as with rock icons such as Metallica or Ozzy Osbourne. But as different as these bands (and the fanbase they attracted) were, what united them was a spirit of anarchy, with backstage and onstage misbehaviour the order of the day. Whether daring Limp Bizkit's Fred Durst to perform naked or luring the underage members of Australian neo-grunge trio Silverchair with alcohol, Korn soon built up a reputation as lethal pranksters. However, their efforts at front-of-house excess weren't always so successful. Fieldy still blushes about the time that excitement got the better of him and he fell off a monitor stack, destroying his precious bass.

The Korn brand was getting exposure, but mainly among committed gig-goers. MTV only dared play their promos in the dead of night – not surprising, given the bleak perspective and the debauching of childhood innocence that permeated the songs and videos. If they were to fulfil their potential, Korn had to translate the intensity of their live show to another studio record.

# CHAPTER 5

# WE HAVE

TAKE-OFF.

Never a band to rest on their laurels or put their feet up, Korn duly ventured back into the studio to record their second album, *Life Is Peachy*. Again they set up camp at Indigo Ranch, with Ross Robinson at the helm.

The record label wanted the group to come up with something quickly, and this additional pressure helped to capture the immediacy and raw spontaneity of a live set. The band rose to the challenge, effortlessly merging structured song-writing with improvised, off-the-cuff interplay and dynamics. This gave the whole performance an energy, vibrancy and evocativeness, unearthing new layers upon each listen.

Released on October 15th, 1996, *Life Is Peachy* debuted at number 3 on the Billboard album chart, confirming the band's standing as mature, groundbreaking artists. Without sacrificing any of the strengths of *Korn*, and even surpassing them in terms of musical ecleticism and risk-taking, the album provided a radical and enthralling blueprint for the new rock sound. The familiar synthesis of funk, hip-hop, grunge, metal and rock was provided here with added force and a visionary spirit, engendering a narcotic mood seething with disillusionment, frustration and, upon occasion, even humour.

An increased budget for recording technology combined with the group's maturing musical skills to create a fuller, fatter and more resonant sound. From the bizarre, barely comprehensible 'Twist' to the grinding 'Good God', Korn had succeeded in pushing their standards to another level entirely. Words, melody, voices, instruments, arrangements and production conspire to formulate a satisfying, multi-focal noise.

The album kicks off in no uncertain terms with the White Zombie-influenced 'Twist', a thundering, metallic melange of sexual phantasmagoria and deranged abandon. Jonathan's maniacal growlings into the microphone aren't exactly a soothing introduction to the delirium of the thirteen tracks to come, owing something to the gruntings of death metal acts like Napalm Death and Extreme Noise Terror. The nihilistic speaking-in-tongues sets the mood perfectly.

With Jonathan's history of alcohol and amphetamine problems, it's surprising that it took until the second album for a song to arrive that explicitly addressed the issue of drug use ('Helmet In The Bush' was more about physical symptoms). The title 'Chi' distances it somewhat from the experiences of Korn, as it's named after Chi Cheng of the Deftones. Jonathan claims this was because the track has a reggae feel and Chi's a big fan of Jamaican music. The "hole" that the narrator digs as a means of escape is presumably the supposed protective hiding of drug-induced anonymity. 'Swallow' also treads over this territory, although it concerns speed-related paranoia. This last track was another that some listeners presumed to be about gay oral sex. Maybe Korn should really do a song on this subject, just to give these people something to chew on. If that's not an unfortunate choice of words...

One of the recurring themes in Korn's lyrics is the transitory nature of non-sexual friendship. Both 'Lost' and 'Good God' are about losing male friends: the first when the friend finds a girlfriend, the second, more bleakly, about someone who turned out to be a leech and an exploiter, who "left me a fucking slave."

'Porno Creep' and 'Mr Rogers' are both about Jonathan's uncomfortable psychosexual experiences as a kid. The original Fred Rogers can best be described as the USA's answer to Brian Cant, a nice old gent in a zip-up cardigan who presented a show with his puppet friends and taught kids basic lessons about honesty and obedience in a friendly, non-threatening manner. Jonathan wasn't the only disturbed five-year-old who found Rogers evil - the sanitised, good-will-triumph world he presented bore no relation to the bullying and abuse the little boy suffered. In a way, it's a return to the themes of 'Shoots and Ladders', in which the happy-go-lucky perfection of children's stories doesn't prepare them for the reality. It is not known if the original Mr Rogers is a Korn fan.

The infamous track, 'K⊕Nº*%!', is explicitly designed to send parents into apoplexy and the band's listeners reaching for the rewind button. Conceived as a litany of blasphemy and foul language, this cut reveals an irreverence, and disregard for conventionality that would separate Korn from their corporate ass-sucking contemporaries. Again, however, it raises questions about Jonathan's attitude to women. He claims "it's not about women in general, just those women who hurt me," but lines like "fuck you, titty-sucking, two-balled bitch with a fat bruised clit" and "Oh shit, fuck, nitch, damn fuckin' diarrhoea slut with HIV" hardly suggest someone who's comfortable with his inner, feminine identity.

The first single from the album, 'No Place To Hide', went on to earn the boys a Grammy Award nomination. It's another tale of childhood betrayal, but rather than confront or attack the bullies and abusers who made his life hell, Jonathan simply asks "why do you make me remember all the hate?"

The majestic, punchy cover of Ice Cube's 'Wicked', featuring The Deftones' Chino Moreno, firmed up Korn's place at the vanguard of rock/rap fusion. "Sitting at the window like Malcolm," a reference to the totemic photo of Civil Rights martyr Malcolm X raises the lyrical stakes from self-pity to a bigger, political sphere.

If there's one consistent criticism of Korn, it's the argument that they don't have a sense of humour. 'Helmet In The Bush' should have seen that one off, but 'A.D.I.D.A.S.' is the track that finally convinced the doubters that Korn can balance their neuroses with a sense of whimsy. Jonathan chants the line, "All Day I Dream About Sex" as if it were a mantra, taking the piss out of all rock stars' aspirations (and that includes the guys from Korn as much as anyone). One of the band's all-time faves and even crediting Jonathan's baby Nathan for additional vocals, it got its own promo video and even made it on to MTV. The video for the song depicts a gruesome car accident involving all five band members and, in a knowing wink to Jonathan's previous occupation, cuts to them laid out on mortuary slabs.

'Ass Itch' is the first song Korn wrote specifically about the process of writing, depicting the pain that Jonathan has to go through simply to get his words down. "I hate writing shit, it's so stupid," he complains, and the agony communicates itself to the listener.

The album climaxes with the bilious hatred of 'Kill You', Jonathan's revenge on his loathed stepmother. Step-parents are potent figures in the fairy stories which inform much of Korn's lyrical content, but even the most twisted creation of the Brothers Grimm would have trouble living down to the ghastliness of this person. Jonathan claims

she laced his tea with Tabasco, and his fevered imagination pictures her "with a knife up your ass", a searing picture of childish revenge.

Jonathan's vocals are powerful throughout the album, gaining a layer of intensity in their wails that hooks the mind, carries you along with his voice as it rises and falls in long, sweeping lines. Sounding like a traumatised young man haunted by dreams, a poet of the common man and a child of the rainbow, Jonathan excels in detailing his wry humour and resilience in the face of despondency. The appeal of his songwriting derives from the universality and purity of his themes: lack of understanding, lack of affection and lack of communication.

The band itself were hitting new surging peaks, as perfectly illustrated by the breezy improvisations of 'Porno Creep' and the head-shattering 'Kill You', which contain as much lyricism and poetry within their grooves as Jonathan's unsparing, stripped-bare words. This album is a record that not only breaks the standard rules and regulations of rock'n'roll, but goes about its business as if they never even existed. Executed as a two-finger salute to the jaded pundits, has-beens and never-wills who claim that nothing new could happen in rock, the album weaves together a rich, sparkling concoction of style and content.

The cover art for *Life Is Peachy* continues the vaguely paedophiliac subtext of *Korn*, depicting a little boy straightening his tie in a gilt mirror whilst another shadowed presence lurks in the background. As for the title of the record, it was inspired by a childrens' popular notebook doodle: "Life is peachy but sex is an all-season sport".

Having by now established a strong world-wide fan base of over two million, Korn kicked off 1997 with a European tour supported by Incubus and Urge. From Hamburg and Bremen through to Glasgow, Wolverhampton, Manchester, Nottingham, Leeds, Newcastle and Bristol, Korn created waves of delirium and ecstasy in the audience with their unstoppable, soulful performances. They continued to spread the gospel in Amsterdam, Copenhagen, Oslo, Stockholm, Berlin, Munich, Vienna, Milan, Toulouse, Marseilles, Madrid, Barcelona, Strasbourg and Paris before returning to Germany.

A rescheduled appearance at London's Brixton Academy on the 24th of February was a landmark one, breaking the venue's records as the entire floor became one massive mosh-pit within a few verses of the boys' opening song. Next up was an all-conquering tour of North America, selling out venues in across the USA before a spell-bounding gig in Toronto, Canada. The tour, with Helmet as support, concluded at the end of March with a concert in Maine.

In the summer, Korn toured Australia and Europe, taking in the Dynamo and Essential festivals, and setting up a live cybercast of their gig at London's Brixton Academy. Confirmation of Korn's burgeoning stature in music arrived when they were invited to perform at Perry Farrell's 1997 Lollapalooza tour.

The concept of Lollapalooza seemed to be tailor-made for a genre-busting band like Korn. Rockers like Tool and Farrell's band Porno For Pyros played alongside rapper Snoop Doggy Dogg and UK dance outfits such as Orbital and Prodigy. Despite the non-metal slant of the bill, the band went down a storm and were mobbed by more than 1,000 fans after the show. However, after completing less than half their scheduled dates, Korn had to abandon the Lollapalooza tour when Munky took ill with a potentially life-threatening case of viral meningitis and was hospitalised. Jonathan issued a statement to the group's fans that explained their decision - they couldn't go on without Munky, it would not feel right. Venues offered refunds for fans who were attending specifically to see Korn play.

Although the guys weren't to know it at the time, it would be more than a year before they would return to live performance.

# CHAPTER 6

# ROCKING IN

THE FREE WORLD

# ROCKIN IN THE FREE WORLD

1998 was a very busy and productive year for Korn. They were working on their third album, but success had given them the resources to channel their creativity into other projects, including their own rock festival, their own record label and even a weekly Internet programme. They also raised eyebrows by signing a $500,000 deal with shoemaker Puma, thereby breaking their long-standing, non-contractual links with the Adidas sportswear company.

On Thanksgiving, they announced the launch of their Elementree Records label. Their first signing was a doom-laden, industrial-influenced outfit known as Orgy. Consisting of singer Jay Gordon, guitarist Ryan Shuck, bassist Paige Haley, and guitarist/synthesiser player Amir Derakh, Orgy had only been together for six months when they signed with Elementree.

The members of Korn were revelling in the freedom and independence of running their own label. Unshackled by record company executives looking over their shoulder, they were left to pick and choose acts with whom they felt a kinship; not only did Orgy feature Ryan Shuck, Jonathan's former bandmate in SexArt, but Elementree's second signing was Cradle Of Thorns, fellow veterans of the Bakersfield scene. Orgy's debut album, *Candyass*, produced by the band with Josh Abraham, was recorded in a massive cabin on a snow-capped mountain in Tahoe. The claustrophobic atmosphere was reflected in the music, which had a tense, raw, malevolent air about it.

Not content with becoming label bosses, Korn also unveiled their Family Values Tour festival, an attempt to translate the eclectic, no-holds-barred atmosphere of summer concerts such as Lollapalooza to an indoor, stadium environment, with the improved sound and lighting that entailed. The line-up was a blend of Korn's protégés, like Limp Bizkit and Orgy, with renegades such as rap titan Ice Cube and controversial German industrial terrorists Rammstein.

The party began on 22nd of September, with tickets costing less than $30 in most cities. To take full advantage of the indoor venues, all the bands paid great attention to the visual aspect of their shows, with a revolving stage installed to cut down time changing between Ice Cube's massive statue of himself and Limp Bizkit's UFO set-up, devised by unhinged guitarist Wes Borland. Rammstein and Orgy, not to be outdone, went to town on superb lightshows.

But there was to be no doubt whose show this ultimately was. As the top-of-the-billers took to the stage, fans were introduced to the Korn Cage, a 45-foot, two-storey giant structure intended to incarcerate fans, some of them competition winners, others randomly selected from the crowd. The Korn Cage enabled the band's fans to share the stage with their idols, not just gaze from below it.

Despite the tour's title, Family Values wasn't submerged in an atmosphere of undiluted peace and love. Rob Zombie, former frontman for White Zombie, was dropped from the bill for reasons that will probably never be resolved to everyone's satisfaction. He claimed it was a purely logistical problem, to do with putting up his stage set: Korn said it was because he didn't want to share a bill with a hip-hop artist. Whatever the truth, Zombie proceeded to set up his own package tour, complemented by a none-more-rock line-up of Fear Factory and Monster Magnet.

As the dust settled, Korn got the full support of Limp Bizkit's Fred Durst and embarked on a promotional Korn Kampaign in 14 cities in as many days, playing live in record stores, signing autographs and doing interviews to promote the forthcoming album. For the Korn Kampaign, the group travelled in a privately chartered jet called Air Korn One. When the band stopped at Greenwich Village, 7,000 fans attended, reputedly the biggest ever in-store in New York. In Toronto, Korn were driven by a tank down a main street, closely followed by some 5,000 kids.

Meanwhile, the band found themselves the subjects of a bizarre rumour regarding a mooted collaboration with Vanilla Ice, the former chart-topper of 'Ice Ice Baby' fame. The Korn camp moved swiftly to dissociate themselves from such an absurd story, assuring their fans that the only Ice to appear on any future Korn release would be Ice Cube. It appeared that Vanilla Ice himself was single-handedly responsible for circulating the rumour. The man known to his mom as Rob Van Winkle reportedly told *The Onion* that he would be working with the group on his new album, *Hard To Swallow*, along with Lenny Kravitz and The Bloodhound Gang. Although, since *The Onion* is a satirical weekly quite capable of spinning the yarn that Irish Protestants were to be deported to Israel, who knows who was pulling whose chain?

Korn were proving to be adept manipulators of press and publicity, but the next chapter in the story came out of the blue. Eric Van Hoven, a student at Zeeland High School in Michigan, was suspended for wearing a Korn T-shirt. What made the case utterly farcical was that the offending garment didn't even carry any of the band's so-called 'obscene' lyrics - the existence of the word 'Korn' was enough (according to school vice-principal Gretchen Plewes) to come under a rule that forbade anything *that might imply* obscenity or anti-social behaviour. Ms Plewes, whose own musical tastes are not recorded, argued that because Korn were "indecent, vulgar, obscene and insulting", any item referring to them must be equally against the rules. In terms of which the vice-principal might not approve, the shit was about to hit the fan with force.

A Grand Rapids radio station, WKLQ, offered free Korn T-shirts outside the school, which drew mass coverage from the local media. A petition drew signatures from hundreds of people - not just rock fans like Van Hoven and his friend Matt Maldonado, who also found himself suspended, but across the whole student body and dozens of parents themselves. MTV, always aware of a good 'them vs. us' story, gave the case blanket coverage. Korn threatened Plewes with legal action, arguing that she had defamed them and that her conduct contravened the First Amendment of the US Constitution in denying Van Hoven the right to free speech. It never came to that, sadly (the thought of Jonathan Davis arguing his case in court is one to savour) but the whole saga sent a message to any doubters that Korn are passionately committed to what they do.

The band continued their plan for media domination with the development of www.korntv.com, which included the online television project KornTV. From 4.30 till 5.30pm each Thursday for eight weeks, the guys communicated with their fans via live calls, tested new material and invited a slew of guest stars into the studio, including Limp Bizkit, Orgy, The Deftones, The Pharcyde and guitar hero Steve Vai, alongside non-musicians like the porn legend Randy Rage. The set was done up like some crazed Middle-eastern harem, with candles and dim lighting adding to the feeling of decadence and fetishism.

The band showed they meant business with the promo trailer for these 'After School Specials', which opened with the line, "Hey fuckers!" It concluded with the equally outrageous "We're gonna blow some shit up!" As well as making their fans feel part of the Korn family, these specials showed a willingness to embrace new technological concepts and incorporate them into their grand vision.

But the band never lost sight of what their number one responsibility to the fans was - the production of the next album.

# SETTING A NEW STANDARD

CHAPTER 7

# SETTING A NEW STANDARD

Anticipation for the band's new album was by this time at a new peak, fuelled by their gushing enthusiasm for the new tracks in interviews leading up to its release. Korn assured their fans that it would be the heaviest thing they'd created to date, setting a new standard for rock.

They took extra time to perfect the sound of the third album, incorporating higher quality sound equipment, re-writing and re-recording material over and over again whenever it was deemed necessary. While still striving to embody the spontaneity and wanton energy of live performance, Korn were reaching for a clarity of production and maturity of songwriting that would once again outshine their contemporaries.

But the increased budgets to which Korn now had access didn't make for a happy artistic environment. The tracks were laid down at NRG studios in North Hollywood and Jonathan stayed at a posh hotel nearby while he wrote the lyrics. The conspicuous consumption and the pretensions of his fellow guests propelled him into an alcohol-fuelled storm of creativity that called up some of his bleakest, most brilliant work.

The guys felt reinvigorated and ready to take a leap into the unknown. At first, Toby Wright's production sounded alien and distorted, but they grew to appreciate that it was just a different way of working from the one they were used to. What appeared uninviting and unusual soon became familiar, comfortable and yet exciting, providing a fresh edge to Korn's music. They recognised that changing things around was vital in keeping things alive as the band were growing musically and creatively as artists.

By now, MTV had finally caught up with the Korn buzz, putting the hits 'Freak On A Leash' and 'Got The Life' on heavy rotation, and creating fevered anticipation for *Follow The Leader* when it was unveiled on the 18th of August 1998. Going straight onto the top of the Billboard album chart, it shifted an incredible 268,000 copies in its first week of release. By now, even the critics were falling into line. *Rolling Stone* magazine praised the album as a work of mastery and invention, awarding it four stars and comparing it favourably to everyone from Black Sabbath and Metallica to Funkadelic and Busta Rhymes. "Prepare to eat shrapnel – whether you like it or not" was the message from critic David Fricke. In addition to this success in the USA, *Follow The Leader* hit the top of the charts in Australia, New Zealand and Canada, number 4 in Finland, 5 in the UK, France and Norway, 8 in Japan, 10 in Holland and 12 in Germany.

Following on from the all-pals-together atmosphere of Korn TV, the record featured an array of special guest appearances from Ice Cube, Trevant Hardson of The Pharcyde, Cypress Hill's B-Real, Fred Durst of Limp Bizkit and, bizarrely, Cheech Marin of 70's stoner comedy duo Cheech and Chong. Perversely,

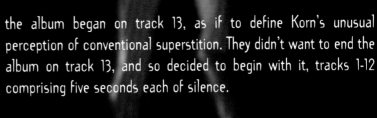

the album began on track 13, as if to define Korn's unusual perception of conventional superstition. They didn't want to end the album on track 13, and so decided to begin with it, tracks 1-12 comprising five seconds each of silence.

The cover artwork for *Follow The Leader*, by Todd McFarlane, was another development of the 'innocent child in peril' motif used on previous Korn albums. It showed a little girl playing hopscotch and jumping off the end of a cliff, followed by a crowd of other children. This haunting image was conceived as a rallying cry, a call to arms for the alternative music scene. Frustrated with the studied apathy, listlessness and wimpiness of much 90's rock and pop, Korn were here calling for a return to depth, meaning and intensity in rock'n'roll. Grunge was OK for a while, but it had soon deteriorated into vacuous, fey, whining adolescent cliché - hello, Pearl Jam! Something with energy, fire and genuine creativity was needed, and Korn were there to provide it.

'It's On' kick-starts the album, a sideswipe at the peer pressure that pushes weak people into drugs and other dubious lifestyle choices. But now Jonathan, rather than flailing wildly at everyone else, looks inside himself and realises "You see it's my fault." The "angels stabbing me inside" aren't the reason he's abusing himself, and they won't be the ones to pull him out of the mess either.

'Freak On A Leash', the video for which went on to pick up two awards at the 1999 MTV Music Video Awards, was a full-on riot of sound, couching Jonathan's diatribe against the record industry. Just as his childhood abuser robbed him of his innocence, so the cut-throat music business is doing it all over again. His success, fame and money has made him feel like a prostitute, "a cheap fuck". For the promo, the guys teamed up with McFarlane and directors Jonathan Dayton and Valerie Faris, combining live action with animation to extraordinary effect.

The first single from *Follow The Leader*, 'Got The Life', was a compelling soundblast of manic, demented rhythms and Jonathan's otherworldly, rumbling moans. There is an image of Jonathan the rock star in dialogue with the Almighty himself where he pours out his innermost feelings of insecurity and discontent to God, who in return reassures him that he is living the life of a king. The accompanying video depicts the trappings of the jet-set rock star lifestyle, with its fast cars, money, worship and adulation. However, the glimpse of Jonathan holding his head in his hands in the back of a limousine signals that all is not well in this supposed new Utopia. His ambivalent feelings towards religion are well-documented - the only truth Jonathan can find is "God beats me."

Dead Bodies Everywhere' gives us more musings on the true nature of the entertainment industry, and gives a clue to Jonathan's maturing perspective as he becomes a father. His dad was a musician, but tried to keep his son out of the business, a stand-off that caused deep and lasting resentment. Now, with the birth of Nathan, David starts to see things through his dad's eyes. But the bitterness still stays: "You really want me to be a good son - why you make me feel like no one?"

Old pal Ice Cube returns to the fray for the fan tribute 'Children Of The Korn', a hymn to "Generation Triple X". Every teenager gets uptight about the older generation telling them "where to skate, who to date, how to fuck, how to kiss, who to love" and this is the rallying call. If any Korn song should give parents a sleepless night, it's this one - an out-and-out challenge to their authority. "Something's gotta' give, parents or the kids - it won't be the kids."

After that excursion into teenage rebellion, it's time for the old Korn staple, a substance abuse song. 'BBK' actually stands for Big Black Cock (nobody said Jonathan could spell), Jonathan's phrase for a Jack Daniels and Coke, one of his favourite tipples. "Take me away, take it away," he sings, unable to decide between drunken oblivion or freedom from his alcoholic crutch.

'Pretty' ranks alongside 'Daddy' as the most raw, agonising songs in the Korn canon. The genesis of it came when Jonathan was working in the coroner's office, and was confronted with the body of an eleven-month-old girl who had been raped and murdered by her father. He has to confront his own feelings of self-pity - however traumatic things get, they're worse for somebody else and wallowing in your own angst ain't going to cure anything.

After that horror, some comic relief is called for. The infectious, rollicking, hip-hop collaboration with Fred Durst, 'All In The Family', is a hilarious, scatological head-to-head, in which each vocalist hurls verbal grenades: "So I hate you and you hate me/It's all in the family" and, best of all, "You call yourself a singer/You're more like Jerry Springer." Other "fuck you" and "suck my dick" references maintain the tongue-in-cheek, adversarial atmosphere on a cut that dispenses with David's drumming in favour of programmed beats. Once again, Korn smudge the boundaries between rock and hip-hop to create something totally fresh and invigorating.

'Justin' was written for one of the group's teenage fans, a fourteen-year-old boy with bowel cancer. Through the Make-A-Wish Foundation, the kid was granted his wish to meet his favourite band in person, and hung out with them during the writing and recording of the song. The whole process forced the members of Korn to re-evaluate their lives and to consider their responsibility to the fans - why was it so special to this dying kid that he wanted to meet these five ordinary guys from Bakersfield? "Time for deep space" indeed...

The self-examination continues in 'Seed', as Jonathan considers his new son and wonders whether he will ever be able to regain the sense of innocence the little guy exhibits. He can justify all the rock star excesses because that's what puts food on Nathan's table. It's just a job - "It's the only thing I really got for now and it's called Fame."

But the gentle, considerate, responsible Jonathan is in eternal conflict with the damaged, bitter, emotional basket-case. 'Cameltosis' is yet another howl of anguish about being hurt by a woman, that degenerates into yet more foul-mouthed abuse.

But it's possible to be too judgmental about these things. The blazing, 15-minute epic, My Gift To You was, superficially, an attempt to write a textbook ballad, but even here Jonathan's dark side couldn't be kept in check. What appeared to be a love letter to his wife, Renée, ends up as a twisted sex-and-murder fantasy, dug up from the murkiest recesses of Korn's leader's consciousness. The news that his wife reportedly loved the song only went to confirm the unconventional nature of their relationship. Maybe Jonathan's attitude to women isn't so twisted after all.

The customary hidden track at the end of the album was a sinister take on the 1978 Cheech And Chong hit, 'Earache My Eye' from the soundtrack to *Up in Smoke*. On this most deranged of cover versions, the band swapped roles: Fieldy contributed lead vocals, Jonathan took over drums and David played bass.

From 'Dead Bodies Everywhere' to 'Children Of The Korn' and 'It's On', *Follow The Leader* is a startling, record, a paradigm shift for Korn, weaving its magic spells on many shifting layers of sound and imagery. Melancholic but brutal, enigmatic but forthright, it speaks volumes of its author. The songs suggest isolation and painful self-awareness, careering from world-weariness through to searing insight.

The album had kept faith with the core ingredients of what can be considered as the generic Korn sound - massive, blood-curdling guitar chords, hellfire vocals, funk-infused rhythmic sensibility - but took it to another dimension of critical and commercial success. Evoking giants such as Black Sabbath, Jane's Addiction, Public Enemy, The Stooges, MC5 and Red Hot Chili Peppers but pursuing their own paths of musical discovery, Korn had finally entered the pantheon of rock legends.

Success was assured, but like the perfectionists they are, Korn continued taking their message to the masses with the never-ending extravaganza that was the Family Values tour. In a stunt of wit and irony that went over many heads, Korn sent a telegram to the USA's former vice-president, Dan Quayle, inviting him to any gig on the Family Values Tour. He was the statesman who had pushed the 'family values' concept to the top of the political agenda, and had become a public laughing stock over his numerous gaffes when he was second-in-command to George Bush Senior in 1988-1992. (Example: when told he was going to Latin America he declared that he'd better brush up his Latin.)

The massive tour concluded on Halloween night in Fairfax, Virginia. To commemorate the last night, all the bands performed in costume. Limp Bizkit became Elvis tributes, Rammstein stripped naked, and, most spectacular Korn demonstrated that, contrary to common belief, they did actually have a sense of humour after all. They dressed up as an spandex-trousered, stack-haired 1980s poodle metal band, churning out covers of Twisted Sister's 'We're Not Gonna Take It' and 'Rock You Like A Hurricane' by The Scorpions. It's not known if the Dee Snider fan club objected to taking their hero's lipstick in vain, but later that night the band narrowly escaped death when a car tried to run the tour bus off the Washington, DC, highway. It could have been the ultimate rock'n'roll death - the whole band perishing in flames on Halloween as a result of creative differences. But there was yet more work to be done, and if an auto crash didn't destroy the band, their own internal pressures were about to have a damned good try.

# CHAPTER 8

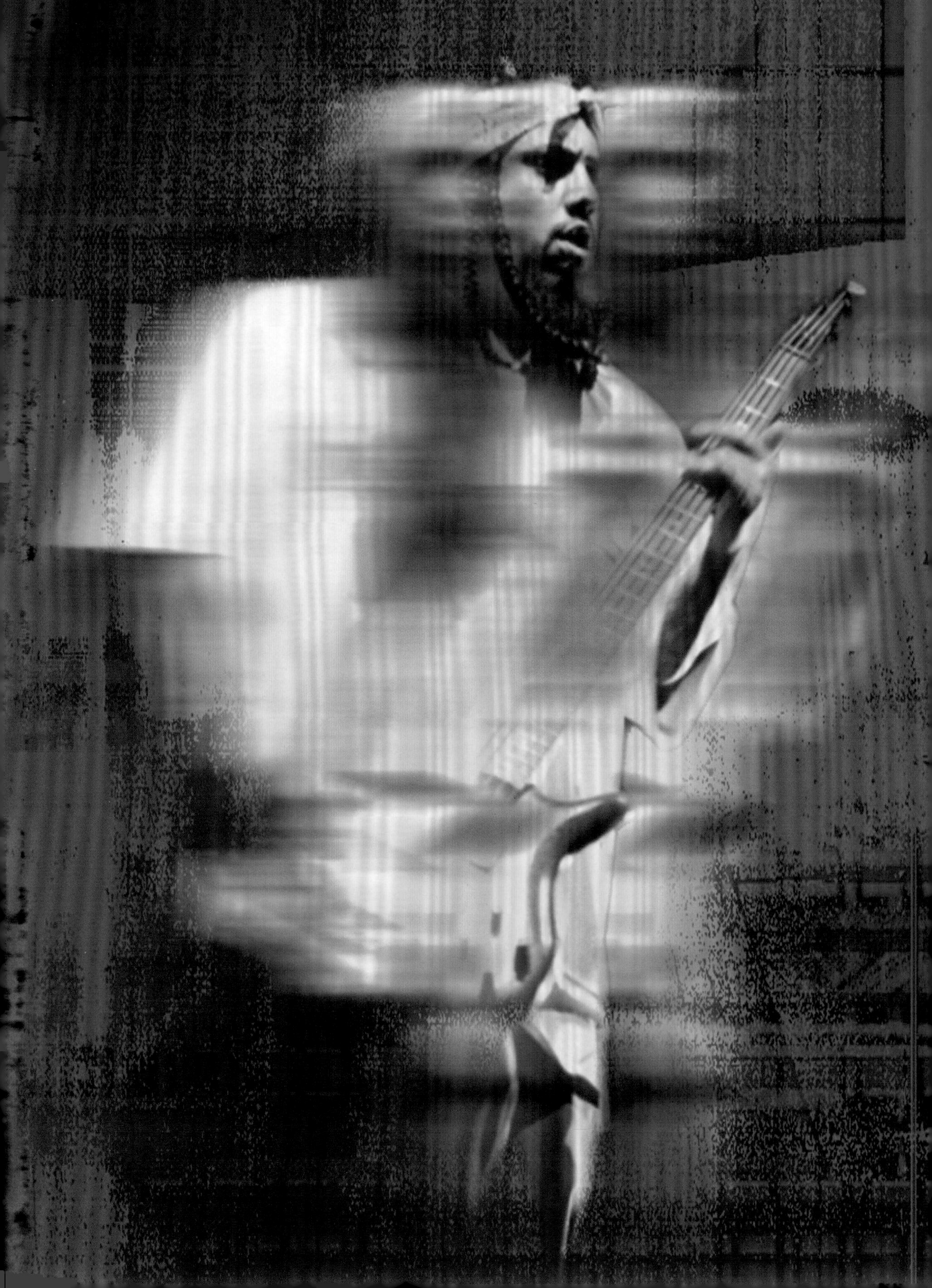

# A GREAT NIGHT IN HARLEM

# A GREAT NIGHT IN HARLEM

In November 1998, Korn's manic schedule finally caught up with them. Moving seamlessly from the insanity of Family Values to a headlining North American tour of their own, something had to give. This time, it was Jonathan who baled out of the Albany, New York, gig, citing nervous exhaustion, although depression and excess drinking probably had as much to do with it.

Incredibly, this was the only date the band cancelled, and they criss-crossed the continent until Christmas. Not content with touring, Jonathan and Renée even found the time to get married. But this wasn't going to be a quick stroll down the aisle in a hired morning suit. For a start, the stag party was organised by porn director Matt Zane, with a supporting cast of fun-loving gals of all shapes and sizes. The wedding itself was less sordid but just as extreme, with medieval decorations and attendant knights and fairies.

After a perfunctory New Year hiatus, they made their first visit to Australia and New Zealand, performing on the Big Day Out tour with Marilyn Manson and Hole. It was a bad-tempered fortnight, with both Manson and Hole leader Courtney Love taking out their personal traumas on the Bakersfield Five. Manson's backbiting was particularly aggravating, as Jonathan had always been up-front in his admiration for the God Of Fuck. If anything, the tour proved that Davis wasn't the only rock front-person whose inner conflicts informed his work.

Korn then spent another three months on their home turf with the ironically-labelled 'Rock Is Dead' tour. Guests included Chino Moreno of the Deftones and old Bakersfield buddies Videodrone, the latest act to be given a leg-up with an Elementree contract. In an effort to rebuild bridges, Rob Zombie was also welcomed back onto the tour – fortunately there were no rap acts around to disconcert him. However, Korn were putting in some serious studio action with the hip-hop fraternity, working with Outkast and Family Values colleague Ice Cube.

A remixed version of 'Freak On A Leash' was donated to the *No Boundaries: Benefit For The Kosovar Refugees* charity record in June 1999, and Korn went down a storm at the ill-fated Woodstock '99 festival. They provided a

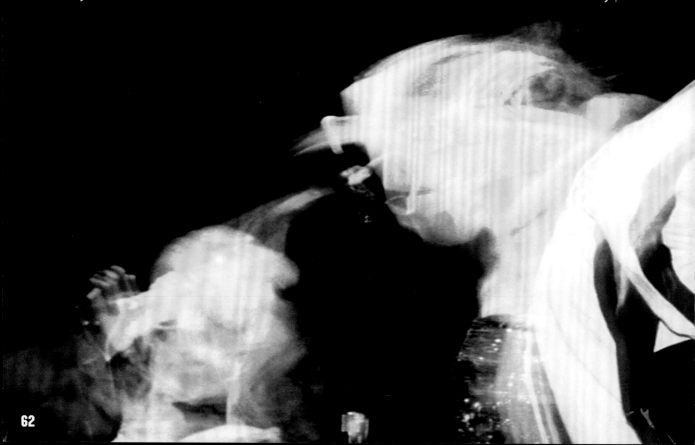

blistering finale to the first day's festivities, and even managed to avoid the critical maelstrom that surrounded Limp Bizkit's Fred Durst when he was accused of provoking a riot. For a change, Korn ended up looking like the good guys. In fact, there was disturbing evidence that Korn were being accepted into the bosom of the music business establishment. The video of 'Freak On A Leash' won two prizes at the MTV Awards and, even more prestigious, beat off the opposition at the Grammys.

Sensibly, Korn took a rest from the pressures of touring after Woodstock. Although they were behind the 1999 Family Values Tour (this time featuring Primus and Staind from the rock camp and DMX, Redman and Run-D.M.C. holding up the hip-hop banner) they elected to return to the studio to prepare their next album, taking occasional breaks to join the Family at selected gigs.

Always keen to explore new avenues in the techniques of self-promotion, the *Issues* album was trailed, not with a conventional single release and promo on MTV, but with a performance by a cartoon version of the band on the cult cartoon show *South Park*. The band even had the ultimate accolade of being the killers of the ill-fated Kenny for this episode. They also released the track as an MP3 via artistdirect.com, who donated 25 cents to children's charities for every download.

To showcase the album, Korn booked the Apollo Theatre in Harlem the night before the November release. The venue is best known for performances by soul and R&B legends such as James Brown, but the Bakersfield boys took to the ambience without problems, with the assistance of Fred Durst, Puff Daddy, Busta Rhymes, a choir and a two police bands. Jonathan made a special effort, looking magnificently ridiculous in his best kilt. The concert was streamed on the internet for those not lucky enough to get a rare-as-hen's-teeth ticket. It was extravagant, it was ludicrous, it was way over the top, but it demonstrated the mental and physical investment that Korn were prepared to make for their music. And the album would back that up.

# CHAPTER 9

BIG

ISSUES

# BIG ISSUES

Unveiled the morning after the big showpiece party in Harlem, the *Issues* album shifted nearly 600,000 units in North America during the first week of release and hit the coveted top spot.

By now the influence of Korn had spread throughout the rock universe, and MTV was heaving with angry young noiseniks, from Limp Bizkit to Kid Rock, giving the world a hard time for the pain they had to suffer. *Issues* had to reclaim the band's position as brand leaders for the genre. It was a searing wide-screen view into the demonic strata of Jonathan's consciousness. The 16 cuts chart the story of its spokesman's descent into hell and his triumphant return to the fray.

The album is like a medieval Mystery play, a journey through paranoia, fragmentation, despair, confusion, rage and dissolution. Yet buried amidst this melange of self-doubt and disillusionment is a glimmer of hope and optimism - partly due to Jonathan ditching alcohol and amphetamines in favour of prescribed anti-depressants such as Prozac. Despite the bleakness of much of the material, it can't be denied that Korn have a sense of humour: it's only a pity that their original idea of naming each track after a different musician was shelved after considering how the legal team for, say, Ricky Martin, might react to being associated with such uncompromising material.

Opening with the stark, whispered mantra "All I want in life is to be happy", 'Dead' could almost be labelled a positive song, in that it identifies the way out of depression and despair. But it ain't that simple - "Every time I get ahead/I feel more dead" complains Jonathan. If he hasn't got his crutch of sadness to cling to, he feels nothing.

But it would be unfair to see Jonathan as a self-obsessed whiner. Sometimes his experiences of, and his reactions to problems can have a positive, outward-looking aspect. For example, 'Falling Away From Me' is a positive stand against domestic abuse, arguing that there is always a way out. "It's gonna be better tomorrow" isn't always the best or most helpful answer.

'Trash' is another relationship-gone-bad anthem, but the blame is placed squarely on the narrator, for falling prey to the charms of groupies. He almost wants rid of his conscience, because his infidelity makes him feel so bad. This feeling of guilt is also covered in 'Make Me Bad', and both songs have a near-biblical emphasis on the weakness of 'the flesh'. Maybe if things had turned out differently Jonathan would have been able to hack it as some sort of hellfire preacher. Although, in a way, that isn't so different from what he does...

In '4U', Jonathan poses the question, "Am I still damned to a life of misery and hate?", but gives thanks for the small miracle that he's still alive, against all the odds. "What you are got me through" he explains, but he's not telling who the "you" is. Some clues might be there when the martial rhythms of 'Beg For Me' herald another tribute to the fans that make the whole Korn experience worthwhile, and a plea to them to "be there for me". 'Wake Up' offers another perspective to the rock'n'roll lifestyle. It's Jonathan's message of thanks to Fieldy, Munky, Head and David, his "brothers" in Korn, a call to arms and a demand that the band "take the stage and remember what we play for".

'Am I Going Crazy' and 'Hey Daddy' are both brutal tracts of self-examination, in which Jonathan wonders whether he's slipped over the fine line between sadness and madness. 'Somebody Someone' takes the process a step further, as he admits that he needs another soul to cling to if he's going to find his way out of the depths - but that somebody will have to share the pain. The constant theme that it might be better to feel that pain than to feel nothing is reiterated in 'No Way'. Is life worthwhile if "anger's the only thing I've made"? Sometimes Jonathan just asks the questions and leaves the answers to the listener.

"Constant paranoia surrounds me.../I fell down in a rut I can't seem to get out of" is the hollow, frank message in 'Let's Get This Party Started', which grows from a funky beginning into a bellowing, throaty blitz of sound. With just about any other band, a title like this would be a chance to let loose, have some fun, maybe knock up a crowd-pleaser that they'll be playing at weddings and bar mitzvahs for the next few decades. But when Korn do it... well, what do you think?

'I Wish You Could Be Me' is another exercise in perspective, and another slingshot at the tormentors who made the adolescent Jonathan's life so vile. It's followed by 'Counting', a fierce, rampant stomp of a tune and yet more relationship-gone-down-the-toilet-never-to-return lyrics. Jonathan's marriage to Renée, rather than making their long relationship more stable, seems to have been more like a kiss of death, and the stress and guilt caused by the couple's separation is etched on the album.

The finale 'Dirty' has a false start of pseudo-jazz elegance before it explodes into the metallic chaos we know and love, offering more nuggets of nihilism: "I feel so bad inside/I wish you could see the world through my eyes/It stays the same/I just want to love again". It's Jonathan at his most vulnerable, calling for salvation. But will he find it in the money-crazed whoredom of the rock business? Watch this space... One of the recurrent themes in the lyrics of *Issues* is an identification with the ever-loyal fans, and an admission that their devotion is what makes all the pain worthwhile. This solidarity with the Korn army was best demonstrated by the fact that the cover was the result of an open competition. The eventual winner was Alfredo Carlos's enigmatic design of a disembodied rag-doll, which netted him $10,000 in the process.

With their thirst for raw freedom of expression, Korn were proving an apposite figurehead for a new style of rock, and their music formed a far more fitting soundtrack to millennial America than drippy grunge or diluted hip-hop. Not only do they express the agony of everyday existence (and latterly, the potential for redemption) but their everything-but-the-kitchen-sink mix of live and sampled sound is a metaphor for the post-modern, multicultural gumbo that is Western society. On *Issues*, tightly constructed arrangements give flesh and colour to Jonathan's lacerating lows and histrionic highs, with some of the finest ensemble playing ever heard on a Korn record. The singer's disembodied voice soars like an eagle and weaves in and out of the group's ever-growing repertoire of licks, riffs, noise and sudden passages of bruised beauty.

The lyrical sophistication of Korn tunes also reached new heights on *Issues*. More and more, they were expanding beyond straightforward love/hate songs or essays of despair, and venturing into philosophical and metaphysical speculations, causing them to be seen as spokesmen for a new generation of adolescents who think too hard; in this, Korn can be seen as the heirs to the likes of Joy Division, The Smiths and Nirvana. For a band that thrives so much on the live experience, almost to the point of self-destruction, it's paradoxical that their albums are better suited to intensive bedroom scrutiny rather than playing one louder on the freeway. *Issues* does not merely invite repeated listenings, it demands them.

This level of lyrical transcendence was exemplified by the promo for 'Falling Away From Me', directed by the band's old buddy Fred Durst. The images of abused children achieving emotional release at a Korn concert was criticised by some as elevating the band to the plane of crypto-Christlike healers. The counter argument is that, to a dysfunctional teenager, rock'n'roll is often the only thing that brings that healing. It was the same argument that had engulfed John Lennon when he claimed the Beatles were bigger than Jesus – it was a reflection on the lack of spiritual fulfilment in modern society, not a cheap shot against the tenets of Christianity.

Critical reaction was mixed. Q magazine described it as "dark, intelligent and very ugly", but *Rolling Stone's* Jon Pareles felt that the group were simply covering old ground, and that, in their over-examination of angst and pain, "the band moves from catharsis to careerism". *NME's* position was somewhere in between, praising 'Let's Get This Party Started' and 'Falling Away From Me' but arguing that musically the album was over-ambitious. 'Make Me Bad' was put out as the second single from *Issues*, accompanied by a Martin Weisz-directed video featuring Brigitte Nielsen and Udo Kier. The track was remixed by Garbage drummer and Nirvana producer Butch Vig, who summed up the conflict of hope and degradation in Korn's lyrics by labelling the reworking 'Sickness in Salvation mix'.

Finally, the band found a few weeks to relax, although Jonathan couldn't divorce himself from work entirely, and recorded a contribution to a tribute album for James Lynn Strait of the band Snot, who had been killed in a car crash in 1998. By February 2000, the urge to perform live had returned, and Korn regrouped for their 37-date Sick & Twisted tour to promote *Issues* throughout North America. Support came from Limp Bizkit protégés Staind and there was even an onstage cartoon show called Spike & Mike's Sick & Twisted Festival of Animation. Ever the innovators, Korn allowed their Web-wise fans to determine the content of some of their set via a poll on www.korn.com.

However, drummer David suffered a recurrence of his previous wrist injury during the North Dakota date on March 10th. The next three shows were postponed, but when the serious nature of the injury transpired, they rescheduled and brought in ex-Faith No More drummer Mike 'Puffy' Bordin to sit behind the kit.

Bordin's stint with the band turned out to be more long-term than anybody had expected, as David was diagnosed with nerve damage. The show went on, and the European tour that culminated in the Netherlands' Pinkpop Festival was an unqualified, resounding triumph for the band. Critics, fans and even jaded old-school rockers had been re-energised by Korn's gut-wrenching sound and never-say-die attitude, not to mention the return of the Korn Kage, in which a few lucky fans were incarcerated every night. This last feature caused some problems for the licensing authorities when the band played at Wembley - it was decided that the capacity should be cut from 40 to 27 and council officials insisted that all participants must go to the toilet beforehand.

In a magazine article in December 2000, Limp Bizkit's Fred Durst was quoted as saying that his band had surpassed the standards of Korn, which provoked a furious, vitriolic response from Jonathan: "Well it's time for me to put that sell-out little bitch in his place. Never bite the hand that feeds". This bitter spat put the cat amongst the pigeons in terms of the two bands' relations, and though Korn's management acted quickly to heal the rift, Jonathan would not confirm whether or not the matter was settled.

Away from matters musical, Jonathan's estranged wife, Renée, sued the Korn frontman, claiming that he was shirking his responsibilities in providing for her and their son, Nathan. In a case that invited delicious media headlines, of the 'Family Values? What Family Values?' variety, Renee argued that her ex was reneging on an agreement that he would pay all her living expenses for the rest of her life. She claimed for half of all Jonathan's accumulated earnings over the 9-year period in which they lived together, insisting that she gave up her career in order to support his. She asked the judge to rule whether or not she was an equal owner of the couple's home, even though they weren't actually married until November 1998. She told the court that before Korn hit the big time, she drove Jonathan to gigs and rehearsals, helped create the band's logo and even had a hand in writing one of Korn's early songs. The lawsuit stipulated that the couple had struck an agreement that Renée would give up work and support Jonathan with the band, ensuring financial stability for life in return. As a result, Renée claimed half of all copyright, royalties, retail and merchandising income earned by her ex-partner over the years.

Further turmoil occurred when Jonathan was at the centre of a sick Internet death hoax at the turn of 2001. Unidentified hackers broke into MTV's News Online site and posted a hoax news-piece that announced the death of the Korn leader. The official band website dismissed the cruel fraud, issuing a statement to confirm that he was very much alive.

The break from live activity gave all the members of Korn the chance to work on other projects. Jonathan, for example, has moved into soundtrack composition, working with Oingo Bongo keyboardist Richard Gibbs to score the film *Queen of the Damned*. Based on the novel by Anne Rice, author of *Interview With The Vampire*, and featuring songs by other artists such as the Deftones, Papa Roach and Tricky, Jonathan has described his musical contribution as "dark gothic kinda tinged", mixing orchestral and rock elements into a frightening modern style. Although Davis sings his compositions during the film itself, due to contractual restrictions he could not appear on the subsequent soundtrack album. Instead, his contributions were re-recorded by artists as diverse as Marilyn Manson, Chester Bennington of Linkin Park and Disturbed's David Draiman. Fieldy, in the meantime, has completed his first solo album called *Rock N Roll Gangster*. Featuring performances from Jonathan Davis and Tre Hardson from Pharcyde amongst others, this hip-hop inspired collection of tracks was released in early 2002, receiving a warm critical reception and showing a side of Fieldy few could have imagined existed. Other band members have even ventured out beyond the musical sphere. David has modelled for Calvin Klein and appeared in the Samo Hung TV show *Martial Law*; Head has gone into business with Orgy's Ryan Shuck, setting up a clothing company called Replicant.

But for all five members, Korn is the number one priority. An appearance alongside The Offspring and No Doubt at the KROQ Weenie Roast in June 2001 was a chance to flex the band's live muscles, but, most importantly, they have been writing and laying down tracks for the new Korn album *Untouchables*. With the projected release date extending from mid-2001 into Spring 2002, information about the album has been severely restricted by the band and those close to them. Produced by Michael Beinhorn who has worked previously with Aerosmith, Marilyn Manson and Hole, Korn have hired top Hollywood directors Albert and Allen Hughes (*Dead Presidents* and *Menace II Society*) to create the video for the first single release *Here To Stay*. With a short South American tour in March 2002 to get their hands in again, Davis and his compatriots are set for a massive US tour and promotional push to support the album's release over the Spring and Summer of 2002.

It is clear, though, that Korn now find themselves at a crossroads. They are the single most influential act in a movement that has revolutionised rock music at the turn of the century, a synthesis of white rock and black hip-hop that has spawned the likes of Limp Bizkit, the Deftones, Blink-182, Linkin Park and many more. They have also taken the traumatised, self-examining lyrical concerns of post-punk acts from Joy Division to Nine Inch Nails and made them resonate on mass-market radio and in stadiums throughout the world. But this success creates problems of its own. How do they progress now that their sound is the sonic currency of the alternative universe? If they keep trudging along the same rut, they'll be just one more rock band - but if they make a radical change, will they still be Korn? A similar conundrum surrounds Jonathan's lyrics. His tales of self-lacerating misery were moving when Korn first arrived, especially among sensitive teenagers for whom they had personal resonance. But he's a big, successful rock star now, with the adulation of millions of fans across the planet, not to mention all the material wealth he could ever dream of. Will another generation of fans take this fucked-up millionaire seriously?

One thing's certain - whatever noise oozes out from the five Bako boys next, it will be cutting in its honesty and beautiful in its deranged ugliness. The definition of un-easy listening, Korn's music isn't for everyone, but devoted fans will lap it up.

# CHAPTER 10

THE KORN METHOD

# THE KORN METHOD

The music of Korn draws upon disparate sources from thrash to metal to funk to hip-hop to rock. But what is this sound, and how do the group go about creating it?

Korn material is conceived very much as a group effort, but invariably Jonathan will sit down with his guitar and come up with some interesting chord progressions, melodies or vocal lines. The genesis of a song then gets given to the other band members, who will invent a series of hooks or riffs and develop them into a piece of music. A multi-layered, complicated track of many strands can be conceived from a single riff. The track is then returned to Jonathan, who will try and work with it and change parts if necessary, for instance if his voice doesn't fit. Lyrics are always left entirely to Jonathan.

When it comes to laying down his inimitable vocals in the studio, Jonathan feels at home if he is surrounded by as many people as possible. With the rest of the band, studio technicians and assorted friends and colleagues spurring him on in the same way as a live audience would, Jonathan can throw himself into the songs as if onstage.

Legend has it that no song ever gets released unless each member of Korn is completely satisfied with it – no part, no cymbal hit, no guitar line escapes the rigorous Korn selection process. This explains why some Korn songs take so long complete, what with the inevitable disagreements, rows and good old musical differences.

Regarding the twin guitar attack of the group, Munky and Head don't have predetermined, roles following the conventional division of 'rhythm and lead'. Many of the guitar parts are shared between the two of them, each taking turns to layer runs over the top of the other's chords. Taking the view that most lead guitar soloing has been done and dusted and can lead to excess and self-indulgence, the band's axe merchants prefer to have the group as a whole build up to a part where each and every musician can enjoy a piece of the lead action. The guitarists aim to set their amps to sound like scratchy AM radios, taking out the bass and adding vintage pedals. Eschewing the sterile modernity of much computer-generated music in favour of the timeless crackle of organic equipment and technology, they prefer the imperfect, raw feel of hip-hop and old crusty funk and soul to the bland, sonic airbrush that sterilises so much modern commercial pop (and even rock).

The other crucial dimension to Korn's guitar sound is the use of Ibanez 7-string instruments, coupled with Head and Munky's idiosyncratic choice of tunings. The wider range of available chords and tonal textures raises the potential breadth of the music way above that of many other bands. While each member actively contributes to the democratic song-writing process, Fieldy wields a significant influence on the band's musical direction and decisions and, as a result, Korn's bass sound is a much more significant part of the mix than it is for some of their contemporaries. Fieldy, who has said that he is "a drummer on bass", also departs from conventionality by not bothering to practise. He never sits mucking around with his bass, preferring to use his instrument only for the serious business of writing tunes. David's beats also have their own character and stylistic traits, with him often plumping for rather high-pitched sounds on both drums and cymbals. Apart from his conventional kit, he also uses a Roland drum machine to enhance his percussive possibilities.

The eclectic nature of Korn's music reflects the taste of its members. Fieldy listens purely to hip-hop from the likes of MC and The Mad Circle, Ice Cube and West Side Connection. One of his biggest heroes as a kid was the electro/hip-hop pioneer, Afrika Bambaataa, whose ground-breaking, seminal single 'Planet Rock' drew him into a new world of beats, cut'n'paste and oral poetry. Not content with planning his own hip-hop album, he has spoken of the prospect of enlisting the production expertise of Dr Dre or The Dust Brothers on a future Korn album, purely because he loves what they do.

David grew up on a variety of music but claims that his biggest musical influence and favourite all-time band are The Bee Gees. Apart from the oeuvre of those sibling harmonists, his most cherished albums include Helmet's *Meantime*, Filter's

*Shortbus*, Urgy's *Candyass*, Blondie's *Greatest Hits* and Weezer's debut long-player. He names 'B.B.K.' as his favourite Korn track. Head is an avowed fan of R&B acts like Boyz II Men, Sublime and Mariah Carey, whilst Munky loves Aerosmith, Faith No More, Mr. Bungle and the legendary funk bassist Bootsy Collins.

Jonathan was, and remains, a huge Duran Duran fan, particularly appreciating the vocals of Simon Le Bon. He has cited as his inspirations Rob Base, Slick Rick, Barry Manilow, Flock of Seagulls, Missing Persons and classical music. He has grown tired of listening to heavy music, although his fondness for the work of Marilyn Manson is unabated. He is particularly fond of Pantera's *Vulgar Display Of Power*, Nine Inch Nails' *Downward Spiral*, Helmet's *Meantime*, Faith No More's *The Real Thing* and *Rio* by Duran Duran. These albums would figure highly amongst his Desert Island choices, but he has also been known to play Lionel Richie's 'Hello' at sound checks and Village People's Greatest Hits collection receives regular airplay on the Korn tourbus.

The Korn show is a remarkable, spiritual odyssey. David never lets up on the kit, contributing faultless, razor-sharp drumming of machine-like efficiency and power, drawing his listeners in like hypnosis. If it has any direct antecedents, it is not the fretwanking virtuosi of conventional heavy metal, but the rhythmic chord-bashers that laid the groundwork for punk – the likes of Bo Diddley, The Stooges and The Who. Munky's homage to The Who's Pete Townshend, a deadpan version of the famous windmill action, takes on a new context of arrogant self-belief.

But the central focus of the group is on the irresistible, charismatic Korn front man and lyricist, Jonathan. Head throbbing violently, hair shaking, body jerking back and forth in time to the relentless beat, his performance is one of abandon, immersion in his craft and complete belief in the affirmative, majestic, uplifting power of the music. Because of the extent to which his inner turmoil has become part of his art, any dysfunctional teen can both identify with him and become part of the rock'n'roll experience. Korn have always gone out of their way to give thanks to their public and the hard-working, hard-partying team behind the scenes of the Korn operation. Constantly amazed by the depth of their fans' knowledge and passion, they always try to imagine themselves in the skin of their followers and so do all they can to reply to queries and hang out back stage. Jonathan is well known for spending hours and hours online communicating with his public. Korn's music provides a release and salvation for kids, a place to visit when things get too much for them.

Those fans have often wondered why it is that none of Korn's albums ever come with a printed lyric sheet, thus depriving them of the pleasure of earnestly scrutinising each and every line whilst listening to their heroes. Jonathan explains that it is a deliberate ploy of the band, as easy access to the words would conspire against the power of the imagination. Left to his or her own devices, with just the music to concentrate on, the listener is more likely to derive his or her own meanings and interpretations. Jonathan is a firm believer in the subjectivity of the musical experience - that we all hear things differently - and feels that lyric sheets constrain the music lover. This hasn't stopped many fans transcribing their own versions of the lyrics and posting them on the internet for the perusal of fellow Kornoholics. The damn near incomprehensible 'Twist' is a particular favourite: "You're not rat dat not then they push take a minute" is just one take on Jonathan's opening salvo.

Korn have always ensured that their support bands are treated as extensions of themselves and not as rivals or competitors, insisting that they receive the same treatment and rights as the headline act, and even helping out with their catering bills upon occasion. Having been impressed by the backstage ambience of the Lollapalooza, they have strived to recreate this at their own concerts, creating a harmonic atmosphere of 'all for one and one for all'. They know from bitter experience that this is a most unusual arrangement, as when they were supporting more established outfits they were invariably treated as second-class citizens by the leading act. Korn's involvement with charity is legendary and has become almost synonymous with the group itself. They are connected with AIDS, leukaemia, Make A Wish, cancer research and child abuse charities and the TJ Martell Foundation Internet Charity Auction. It's just one of many paradoxes and enigmas that surround the band – their doom-laden lyrics and demonic stage shows seem to be in direct contradiction of their humanitarian concerns.

# CHAPTER 11

# A NEW BALANCE

# A NEW BALANCE

Amidst the frenzy of rock'n'roll immortality, it is sometimes easy to forget that each member of Korn has his own distinctive personality and unique take on life. The beauty of Korn's success lies somewhere between the unflagging group camaraderie, and the individual components brought by each member. So what is that drives the members of Korn?

Fieldy is known for wearing his heart on his sleeve and being unafraid to display his emotional and sensitive side. In fact, he can blub over almost anything, no matter how profound or corny. He can cry when watching the band's performances on video tape or when viewing The Lion King or some such Disney blockbuster. The intensity of life on the road can likewise induce sporadic bouts of tears in Fieldy, but can also just as easily result in him vomiting. For instance, when the lights go out and the band's name is announced, he can puke through sheer nervous energy and excitement.

The adrenaline-junkie bass maestro has never been one for the heavy drug consumption favoured by most rock legends. Having experimented with a bit of cannabis in his teens and never seeing the point of it, he realised early on that beer was his vice of choice, though he has been known to take the odd sedative. His alcohol consumption on the Who Then Now? video is of titanic proportions. Yet Fieldy now knows where to draw the line, and a lot has changed since his marriage to Shela and the births of his two children, Serena Rae and Olivia.

Fieldy, a long-time aficionado of sushi, has had his personal differences with other band members over the years, particularly with David and Head, but has always managed to reconcile them. On one occasion, a row with David happened to have been recorded on a tape recorder by Munky, and the resulting playback convinced them of how moronic and ridiculous they had been. One confrontation with Head resulted in Fieldy dragging him by the leg down a street. Fortunately, as he has matured, these incidents are now extremely rare and any discord within the camp tends to be dealt with in an adult manner.

As well as his immense musical contribution to the group, Fieldy designs all official Korn merchandise - hats, stickers and T-shirts. All of his designs have to be vetoed by the rest of the guys before they get the all-clear.

The nipple-pierced, tattooed drumming sensation David has developed a rather lucrative sideline in modelling and acting. He has completed modelling assignments for the skatepunk clothing companies 26 Red and Grind as well as Calvin Klein, and has appeared in the cop show, Martial Law. His personal life has fortunately been free of major upheavals and angst, having married his girlfriend Shannon Bellino in April 1997 and seeing his son, David Jr., born on August 22nd, 1997.

David's love of tattoos has been well documented: he has one of his wife's first name along his back and three more on other parts of his body. These are of a Cheshire cat, a guy sticking out a drum stick-encrusted tongue and the band's famous logo. His famous penis fetish has become a defining feature - in fact, whenever he gives his autograph or signs any document he often doodles one alongside his name. He tends to steer clear of the drink, and he adopts a strict work-out regime when not on tour in order to keep in shape. He has to keep fit and alert as he has no choice but to keep his limbs moving at the drumkit.

Virtuoso axe man and *Simpsons nut*, Head, is a party animal but restricts his allegiance to alcohol. He claims to know when to quit, unlike other members of Korn, and prefers the American variety to the European kind. Head, who contributes backing vocals to many tracks, is also a family man and is totally committed to his wife Rebekah and their daughter Jennea Marie, who was born on the 6th of July, 1998. He refused to travel overseas whilst his wife was pregnant, and Korn had to pull out of the European Ozzfest of 1998 because she was due to give birth at any moment.

Guitar wizard Munky, a long-time fan of The Incredible Hulk and The Pharcyde, loves the buzz of being in a groundbreaking rock band, but admits that there have been times when the pressure and intensity have taken their toll. After some shows, he has to lock himself in the bathroom and cry because he feels so exhausted by the Korn phenomenon. His bout of life-threatening viral meningitis refocused his life and encouraged him to appreciate the beauty of what he had when he recovered and hooked up with the band again. Away from the group, he loves playing with his Sony Playstation and driving his Mercedes E320.

Korn's leader and enigmatic frontman, Jonathan, brought a lot of baggage to the band and looks upon his music as a means of emotional and spiritual catharsis. Whether it be the pain of his parents' split, his suffering abuse as a child, his alcohol and drug problems or the post-traumatic stress disorder suffered from his days as an assistant coroner, he has certainly had a lot to contend with. And yet you can't escape the feeling that without this litany of impoverishment and dysfunction, the music world would have been deprived of the Korn success story.

Although nowadays he claims to only touch alcohol, Jonathan's history of drug consumption is a somewhat chequered one. He claimed to have spent a whole two-year period without sleep, thanks to his prolific drug intake. He has alluded to ingesting methamphetamines and having sex with his girlfriend in his car whilst out of his mind on speed.

But alcohol has long been his major vice, at times just for the sheer hell of it, but more often to escape from the boiling hot cauldron of rock'n'roll fame. He once said that he couldn't get by without alcohol in his system as

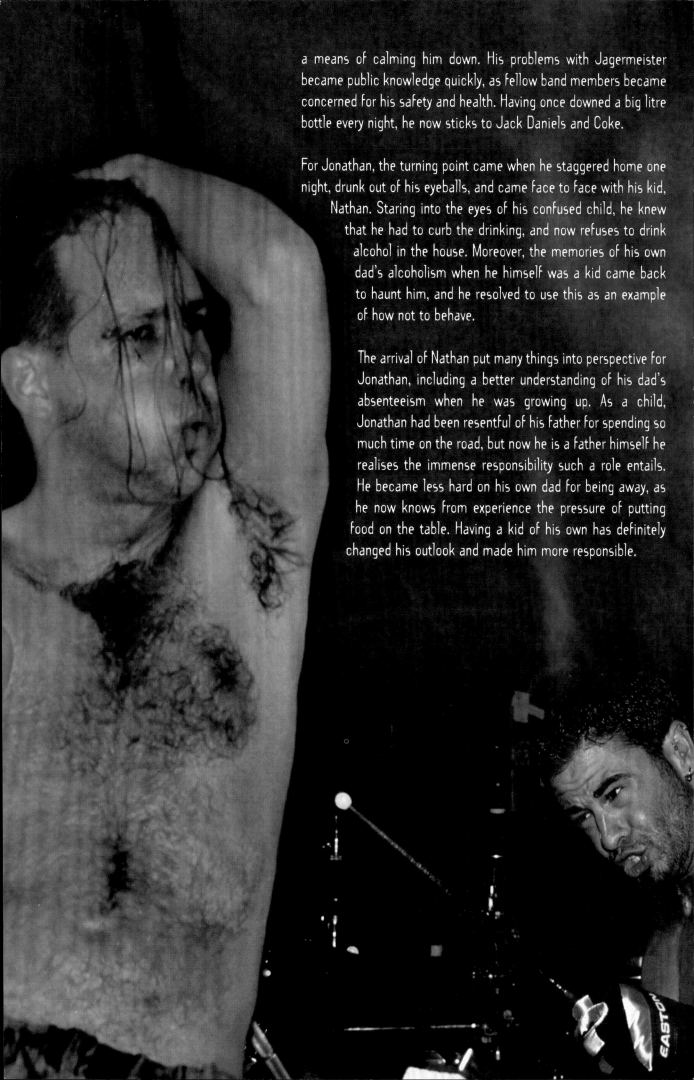

a means of calming him down. His problems with Jagermeister became public knowledge quickly, as fellow band members became concerned for his safety and health. Having once downed a big litre bottle every night, he now sticks to Jack Daniels and Coke.

For Jonathan, the turning point came when he staggered home one night, drunk out of his eyeballs, and came face to face with his kid, Nathan. Staring into the eyes of his confused child, he knew that he had to curb the drinking, and now refuses to drink alcohol in the house. Moreover, the memories of his own dad's alcoholism when he himself was a kid came back to haunt him, and he resolved to use this as an example of how not to behave.

The arrival of Nathan put many things into perspective for Jonathan, including a better understanding of his dad's absenteeism when he was growing up. As a child, Jonathan had been resentful of his father for spending so much time on the road, but now he is a father himself he realises the immense responsibility such a role entails. He became less hard on his own dad for being away, as he now knows from experience the pressure of putting food on the table. Having a kid of his own has definitely changed his outlook and made him more responsible.

Jonathan's episodes of depression and suicidal angst have been a prominent feature throughout Korn's rise to the top. The first Family Values tour, in particular, was a hellish time for the lead vocalist. Onstage, he felt like a God, drowning in the adulation of his followers and getting high from the spirit of the music, but off stage he was a mental wreck, entertaining thoughts of ending it all and staying in bed all day, deeply depressed.

Nowadays, Jonathan's mental psyche is healthier and more settled, in part thanks to his increased responsibility and maturity, in part because of the success of his medication, a cocktail of Prozac and Dexedrine. The medication has helped to correct a chemical imbalance in his brain that made him freak out and lose the plot on many occasions. However, Jonathan has accepted that a degree of angst is still necessary to keep the band interesting and evolving. Releasing his demons into his art - for a couple of hours on stage or even for the duration of the recording sessions - is still the most productive form of therapy he knows, and he has learnt to harness his more destructive tendencies for the most part in his personal life. It is an awkward balance, but one which Jonathan seems to have pulled off.

# CHAPTER 12

# FROM THE DEPTHS: THE THOUGHTS OF JONATHAN DAVIS

# FROM THE DEPTHS: THE THOUGHTS OF JONATHAN DAVIS

"People die from typewriters falling on their heads."

"Cheesy pop songs just bore me to death."

"Real friends stab you in the front."

"We're not trying to change the world - just music."

"I don't know the true meaning of happiness."

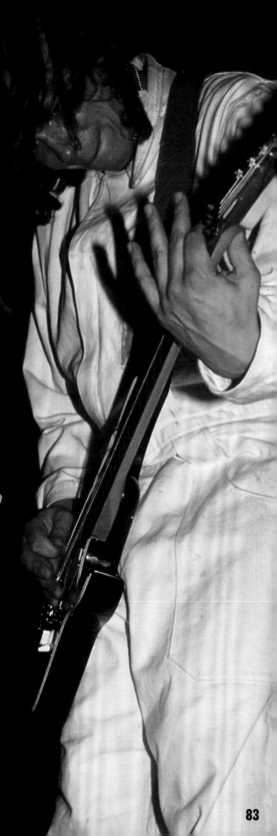

"When you're really depressed it's good to hear someone be hurt too."

"When I listen to music I don't want to hear about flowers. I like death and destruction."

"When I get depressed I listen to my own fucking music."

"The music industry can make you feel like a prostitute."

"I don't care what people think or say about me – I know who I am."

"You laugh at me because I'm different – I laugh at you because you're all the same."

# DISCOGRAPHY

# DISCOGRAPHY

ALBUMS

**Korn:** *Blind / Ball Tongue / Need To / Clown / Divine / Faget / Shoots And Ladders / Predictable / Fake / Lies / Helmet In The Bush / Daddy*
LP/CD/CASS - Immortal/Epic Records 1994

**Life Is Peachy:** *Twist / Chi / Lost / Swallow / Porno Creep / Good God / Mr. Rogers / K@#*%! / No Place To Hide / Wicked / A.D.I.D.A.S. / Low Rider / Ass Itch / Kill You*
LP/CD/MINI-DISC/CASS - Immortal/Epic Records 1996

**Follow The Leader:** *It's On / Freak On A Leash / Got The Life / Dead Bodies Everywhere / Children Of The Korn / B.B.K. / Pretty / All In The Family / Reclaim My Place / Justin / Seed / Cameltosis / My Gift To You* – Also avaliable with a bonus second CD containing *All In The Family (Clark World Mix) / All In The Family (Sowing The Beats Mix) / All In The Family (Beats In Peace Mix) / All In The Family (Scary Bird Mix)*
LP/CD/CASS - Immortal/Epic Records 1998

**Issues:** *Dead / Falling Away From Me / Trash / 4 U / Beg For Me / Make Me Bad / It's Gonna Go Away / Wake Up / Am I Going Crazy? / Hey Daddy / Somebody Someone / No Way / Let's Get This Party Started / I Wish You Could Be Me / Counting / Dirty* - CD also available with limited edition MTV Competition Winners' sleeves. Also available as a promo CD featuring *Falling Away From Me / Trash / Beg For Me / Wake Up / Let's Get This Party Started* and as a 2CD set featuring *A.D.I.D.A.S. (Radio Mix) / Good God (Dub Pistol Mix) / Got The Life (Josh Abraham Mix) / Twist/Chi (Live) / Jingle Balls*
LP/CD/CASS - Immortal/Epic Records 1999

SINGLES

US SINGLES:

**Blind** - US Promo Release
VINYL - Epic/Immortal 1994

**Need To** - US Promo Release
VINYL/CD - Epic/Immortal 1994

**Clown:** *Clown (Radio Edit)* - US Promo Release
VINYL/CD - Epic/Immortal 1995

**Shoots And Ladders:** *Shoots And Ladders (Radio Edit) / Sean Olson (Radio Edit)* - US Promo Release
VINYL/CD - Epic/Immortal 1995

**A.D.I.D.A.S.:** *A.D.I.D.A.S. (Synchro Dub) / A.D.I.D.A.S. (Under Pressure Mix) / A.D.I.D.A.S. (The Wet Dream Mix) / Wicked (Tear The Roof Off Mix)*
12" VINYL - Epic/Immortal 1996

**A.D.I.D.A.S.:** *A.D.I.D.A.S. (Radio Edit)* - US Promo Release
VINYL/CD - Epic/Immortal 1996

**All In The Family:** *All In The Family (Album Version) / All In The Family (Clark World Remix) / All In The Family (Sowing The Beats Mix) / All In The Family (Beats In Peace Mix) / All In The Family (Scary Bird Mix)* - US Promo Release
VINYL - Epic/Immortal 1998

**Got The Life:** *Got The Life / Got The Life (Deejay Punk-Rock Mix / Got The Life (D.O.S.E. Wollyback Remix) / I Can Remember*
CD - Epic/Immortal 1998

**Got The Life:** *Got The Life / Got The Life (Deejay Punk-Roc Remix)*
VINYL - Epic/Immortal 1998

**No Place To Hide:** *No Place To Hide / Sean Olson / Lies*
VINYL/CD - Epic/Immortal 1998

**Good God:** *Good God / Good God (Remix) / Need To (Live) / Divine (Live)*
VINYL/CD - Epic/Immortal 1998

**Christmas Song:** *Christmas Song (Blatant FCC Violation version) / Christmas Song (Squeak by the FCC version)*
RED VINYL 12" - Epic/Immortal 1998

**All Mixed Up:** *A.D.I.D.A.S. (Radio Mix) / Good God (Dub Pistols Mix) / Got The Life (Josh Abraham Remix) / Twist/Chi (live)*
VINYL/CD - Epic/Immortal 2001

UK SINGLES:

**Blind:** *Blind / Fake / Sean Olson*
10" VINYL - Epic/Immortal 1995

**No Place To Hide:** *No Place To Hide (Album Version) / Sean Olson / Proud (previously unreleased)*
CD - Epic/Immortal 1996

**No Place To Hide:** *No Place To Hide (Album Version) / Shoots And Ladders (Hip-Hop Mix) / Shoots And Ladders (Industrial Mix)*
CD - Epic/Immortal 1996

**No Place To Hide:** *No Place To Hide (Album Version) / Proud (previously unreleased)*
7" VINYL - Epic/Immortal 1996

**A.D.I.D.A.S.:** *A.D.I.D.A.S. (Radio Edit) / Chi (Live) / Ball Tongue (Live) / Lowrider / Shoots And Ladders (Live)*
CD - Epic/Immortal 1996

**A.D.I.D.A.S.:** *A.D.I.D.A.S. (Album Version) / Faget / Porno Creep / Blind*
CD - Epic/Immortal 1996

**A.D.I.D.A.S.:** *A.D.I.D.A.S. (Radio Edit) / Chi (Live) / Lowrider / Shoots And Ladders (Live)*
12" VINYL - Epic/Immortal 1996

**Good God:** *Good God (Album Version) / Good God (Mekon Mix) / Good God (Dub Pistols Mix) / Wicked (Tear The Roof Off Mix)*
CD - Epic/Immortal 1996

**Good God:** *Good God (Album Version) / A.D.I.D.A.S. (Synchro Dub) / A.D.I.D.A.S. (Under Pressure Mix) / A.D.I.D.A.S. (The Wet Dream Mix)*
CD - Epic/Immortal 1996

**Good God:** *Good God / Good God / A.D.I.D.A.S. / A.D.I.D.A.S.*
12" VINYL - Epic/Immortal 1996

**Good God:** *Good God / Good God (Heart Floor Remix) / Good God (Headknot Remix) / Good God (OOMPH! vs. Such A Surge Mix) / Good God (Mekon Mix) / Good God / Dub Pistols Mix)*
CD - Epic/Immortal 1996

KORN
peaches
korn

KORN All Mixed Up

KORN
iSSUES

KORN Lif

FAMILY VALUES
THE BIGGEST SHOW OF STARS TOUR
KoRn
RAMMSTEIN
ICE CUBE
Limp Bizkit
OrGy
A ROCK N' ROLL EXTRAVAGANZA!

KoRn
pRouD tO beAgAin!
A COLLECTION OF RARE AND UNRELEASED TRACKS

BIG DAY OUT

KoRn

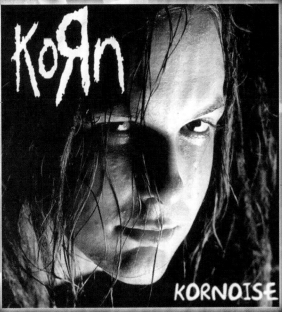
KoRn

KoRn

KoRnoise

87

**Good God:** *Good God / Good God (Live) / Need To (Live) / Divine (Live)*
CD - Epic/Immortal 1997

**Got The Life:** *Got The Life / Got The Life (Deejay Punk-Roc Remix) / Got The Life (D.O.S.E. Woollyback Remix)*
CD - Epic/Immortal 1998

**Got The Life:** *Got The Life / I Can Remember / Good God (OOMPH! vs. Such A Surge Remix)*
CD - Epic/Immortal 1998

**Got The Life:** *Got The Life (Deejay Punk-Roc Remix) / Got The Life (D.O.S.E. Woollyback Remix) / Got The Life*
12" VINYL - Epic/Immortal 1998

**Freak On A Leash:** *Freak On A Leash (Album Version) / Freak On A Leash (Dante Ross Mix) / Freak On A Leash (Freakin' Bitch Mix) (aka Butch Vig Mix) / Freak On A Leash (Josh A's Beast On A Leash Mix) / Freak On A Leash (Lethal Freak Mix)*
CD - Epic Immortal 1998

**Make Me Bad:** *Make Me Bad / Dirty (Live) / Make Me Bad (Live) / Make Me Bad (CD-ROM Video)*
CD - Epic/Immortal 1999

**Make Me Bad:** *Make Me Bad / Dirty (Live) / Make Me Bad (Live) / Make Me Bad (Sybil Mix) / Make Me Bad (Sickness in Salvation Mix) / Make Me Bad (Kornography Mix)*
CD - Epic/Immortal 2000

**Falling Away From Me:** *Falling Away From Me (Radio Edit) / Jingle Bells / Falling Away From Me (Accapella)*
CD - Epic/Immortal 2000

**Falling Away From Me:** *Falling Away From Me / Falling Away From Me (Remix) / Got The Life (Remix)*
CD - Epic/Immortal 2000

AUSTRALIAN SINGLES:

**Good God:** *Good God (Clean Version) / Need To (Live) / Good God (Album Version) / Good God (Heartfloor Mix) / Divine (Live) / Good God (Such A Surge Remix)*
CD - Epic/Immortal 1996

**Got The Life**
CD - Epic/Immortal 1996

**Freak On A Leash:** *Freak On A Leash / Freak On A Leash (Freakin' Bit*h Mix) / Freak On A Leash (Josh A's Beast On A Leash Mix) / Freak On A Leash (Lethal Freak Mix) / Freak On A Leash (Dante Ross Mix).*
CD-ROM - Epic/Immortal 1998

**Falling Away From Me**
CD - Epic/Immortal 1999

EUROPEAN / INTERNATIONAL SINGLES:

**No Place To Hide:** *No Place To Hide (Album Version) / Sean Olson (Radio Edit) / Lies*
VINYL/CD/CASS - Epic/Immortal 1996

**Shoots And Ladders:** *The Dust Brothers Remixes: Hip-Hop Remix / Hyper Remix / Industrial Remix / Industrial Instrumental*
VINYL - Epic/Immortal 1996

**Falling Away From Me:** *(Parts One And Two)*
CD - Epic/Immortal 1999

**Make Me Bad:** *Make Me Bad / Dirty (Single Mix) / Make Me Bad (Single Mix) / Make Me Bad (Sickness In Salvation Mix) / Make Me Bad (Danny Saber's Remix) / Make Me Bad (Kornography Mix) / Make Me Bad (Sybil Mix)*
CD - Epic/Immortal 1999

FRENCH SINGLES:

**Good God French Remixes:** *Good God (Marc Em Remix) / Good God (Oneeyed Remix Krinick Bass) / Good God (Headknot Remix) / A.D.I.D.A.S. (Synchro Dub) / Good God (Album Version)*
CD/VINYL - Epic/Immortal 1997

**Freak On A Leash:** *Freak On A Leash (Album Version) / Freak On A Leash (Dante Ross Remix) / Freak On A Leash (Freakin' Bitch Mix) / Freak On A Leash (Josh A's Beast On A Leash Mix) / Freak On A Leash (Lethal Freak Mix), Freak On A Leash (One Shot Remix).*
CD - Epic/Immortal 1998

GERMAN SINGLES:

**A.D.I.D.A.S.**
CD - Epic/Immortal 1997

**No Place To Hide:** *No Place To Hide / Proud / Lies*
VINYL/CD/CASS - Epic/Immortal 1997

**Got The Life:** *Got The Life / Got The Life (Vorticist's Suite) / Got The Life (I Got A Knife) / Children Of The Korn (Clarkworld Remix)*
CD - Epic/Immortal 1997

## COMPILATIONS / SOUNDTRACKS:

**X-Games, Volume 1.**
CD - Tommy Boy Records 1996

**The Crow: City Of Angels:** *Sean Olson*
CD - Hollywood Records 1996

**I Know What You Did Last Summer:** *Proud*
CD - Sony Records 1997

**Spawn:** *Kick The P.A. (With The Dust Brothers)*
CD - Epic Records 1997

**Devil's Jukebox:** *Got The Life (D.O.S.E. Woollyback mix)*
CD - Free with Kerrang! Magazine 1998

**Rock Sound Sampler:** *All In The Family (edit)*
CD - Free with Rock Sound magazine 1998

**No Boundaries - A Benefit For The Kosovar Refugees:** *Freak On A Leash*
CD - Epic Records 1999

**Woodstock '99:** *Blind*
CD - Epic Records 1999

**End Of Days:** *Camel Song*
CD - Geffen Records 1999

**MTV: Return Of The Rock:** *Make Me Bad (Butch Vig Sickness In Salvation mix)*
CD - 1999

**Family Values: The Biggest Show Of Stars For '98:** *Shot Liver Medley (Shoots And Ladders / Justin / Predictable / Ball Tongue / Divine / Kill You) / Freak On A Leash / Twist-Chi / Got the Life*
CD - Immortal/Epic Records 1999

**Family Values Tour 1999:** *Falling Away From Me / A.D.I.D.A.S. / Good God / Flawless*
CD - Geffen Records 2000

## GUEST APPEARANCES

**Sepultura: Roots:** *Look Away / Ratamahatta (vocal by Jonathan Davis)*
CD - Roadrunner 1996

**Ice Cube: War And Peace (vol 1):** *Fuck Dyin'*
CD - Priority 1998

**Orgy: Candyass:** *Revival*
CD - Elementree 1998

**Limp Bizkit: Significant Other:** *Nobody Like You (vocal by Jonathan Davis)*
CD - Flip/Interscope 1999

**Various Artists: Strait Up:** *Take It Back (vocal by Jonathan Davis)* - Tribute album to the late James Lynn Strait of the band Snot.
CD - EMD/Virgin 2000

**Videodrone: Videodrone:** *Ty Jonathan Down / Power Tools For Girls*
CD - Elementree 2000

**Q-Tip: Amplified:** *End Of Time*
CD - LaFace 2001

**Deadsy: Commencement:** *Sleepy Hollow (vocal by Jonathan Davis)*
CD - Elementree 2001

## BOOTLEGS

Bootlegs are unofficial releases of mixes, live recordings, downloads and rare tracks. There are numerous CDs around featuring Korn, and below is a selection of the most common ones. It should be noted that to sell or trade in bootleg material is a criminal offence, therefore they are only available from underground sources such as market stalls and record fairs. The authors and publishers of the book do not endorse any trade in such items nor do they have any further information about their availability.

As Fieldy said, "Bootleggers are making more money than us!"

**Proud Again** - *I Can Remember / Lookaway* (Sepultura featuring Jonathan Davis) / *Power Tools For Girls* (Videodrone featuring Brian 'Head' Welch) / *Ty Jonathan Down* (Videodrone featuring Jonathan Davis) / *Revival* (Orgy featuring Jonathan Davis) / *Good God (Marc Em Remix)* / *Freak On A Leash (One Shot Remix)* / *Got The Life (Josh Abraham Remix)* / *All In The Family* (Live With Limp Bizkit) / *Children Of The Korn* (Live With Ice Cube) / *A.D.I.D.A.S. (Live)* / *Faget (Live)* / *Revival (Live)* / *Children Of The Korn (Clarkworld Remix)* / *All In The Family (Clarkworld Remix)* / *Black Sheep (Live)* / *Jingle Bells (Live)*

**Going Crazy In Trash City** - *Intro (Pipe and Drum Chor Of The NYC Police Department)* / *Falling Away From Me / Trash / 4 U / Beg For Me / Make Me Bad / It's Gonna Go Away / Wake Up / Am I Going Crazy / Hey Daddy / Somebody Someone / No Way / Let's Get This Party Started / Wish You Could Be Me / Country / Dirt* (Above Tracks Recorded Live At The Apollo Theatre NYC November 14th 1999) - *It's On / Freak On A Leash / Twist / Chi / A.D.I.D.A.S. / Shoots And Ladders / Blind* (Above Tracks Recorded Live At The Royal Melbourne Showground, Melbourne Australia Jan 26th 1999)

**Kornography** - *Kick The Pa* (Featuring The Sneaker Pimps) / *A.D.I.D.A.S. (Wet Dream Mix)* / *Wicked (Tear The Roof Off Mix)* / *Sean Olsen (Edit)* / *Proud / Alive (1994 Demo) / Need To* (Live In The USA March 1997) / *Divine* (Live In The USA March 1997) / *Christmas Song (F.C.C. Version)* / *This Town (Fuck The F.C.C. Version)* / *A.D.I.D.A.S. (Radio Mix)* / *Predictable (Early Demo Version)* / *Daddy (Early Demo Version)* / *Good God (Marc Em Remix)* / *I Can Remember / Ball Tongue* (Live In Dallas, 23 November 1996) / *Low Rider / Shoots & Ladders* (Live In Dallas, 23 November 1996)

**Family Forum** - *Shoots & Ladders / Blind / Freak On A Leash / 'Twas The Night Before Xmas / Got The Life / My Gift To You / Jingle Bells* (Above Tracks recorded at L.A. Shrine Auditorium 12/11/98) / *Shoots & Ladders / Justin / Ball Tongue / B.B.K. (Big Black Kock) / Blind / Got The Life / Dead Bodies / Faget / All In The Family* (with Fred Durst on Guest Vocalist) (Above Tracks Recorded Live At The L.A. Forum 1998)

**Peaches & Korn: Live In Philadelphia 1997** - *No Place To Hide / Twist / Blind / Chi / Interview With Jonathan / A.D.I.D.A.S. / Good God / Low Rider / Shoots & Ladders / Interview Part 2 / Divine / Ass Itch / Interview Part 3 / Kill You / Faget / A.D.I.D.A.S. (Radio Edit) / Chi / Ball Tongue / Shoots & Ladders*

**Children Of The Korn** - *Blind / Ball Tongue / Divine / Chi / Low Rider / Shoots & Ladders / Good God / Faget* (Above Tracks Recorded Live at K-Rog Wienie Roast) / *Proud / Sean Olsen / Shoots & Ladders (Industrial Mix) / Shoots & Ladders (Country Mix) / Shoots & Ladders (Trip Hop Mix) / Shoots & Ladders (Hip Hop Mix) / Predictable* (Above Tracks All Studio Demos)

**Kornnoize - The Electric Factory, Philadelphia, November 1996** (Plus Demos) - *Twist / Blind / Chi / A.D.I.D.A.S. / Good God / Shoots & Ladders / No Place To Hide / Divine / Ass Itch / Kill You / Faget / Predictable (demo) / Blind (demo) / Daddy (demo) / Alive (demo) / Xmas Song / Sean Olson / Proud*

**Kornoise - Life Is Peachy Tour, California, March 1997** - *Intro / Twist / Blind / Chi / Need To / Good God / Clown / Ball Tongue inc. / We Like To Party / A.D.I.D.A.S. / Lowrider / Shoots & Ladders / No Place To Hide / Swallow / Fake / Divine / Kill You / Faget / A.D.I.D.A.S. (Alternate Version) / Xmas Song (Unreleased Demo '94)*

**Big In Japan** - *It's On / Freak On A Leash / Twist / Chi / Reclaim My Place / Need To / A.D.I.D.A.S. / Medley – Justin/Preceivcatable/Ball Tongue/Divine/Proud / Kill You / Blind / Got The Life / Dead Bodys Everywhere / My Gift To You / Faget / Earche My Eyes*

**Trashin' Bagpipe** - *Blind / Ball Tongue / Divine / Need To / Clown / Good God / Shoots & Ladders / Lies / Daddy / Fake / Faget* (Above Tracks Recorded Live At The Astoria, London, August 22 1996) / *Good God / Shoots & Ladders / Interview* (Above Tracks Recorded Live At The Donnington Festival, UK, August 17 1996)

**Korn** - *Blind / Twist / Chi / Got The Life / Good God / A.D.I.D.A.S. / Shoots & Ladders / New Song / Freak On A Leash / New Song / Faget / New Song* (Above Tracks Recorded Live At The Woodstock Festival NY, USA, July 23rd 1999) / *It's On / Kill You / B.B.K.* (Above Tracks Recorded Live at The Big Day Out Festival Melbourne, Australia, January 26th 1999)

**Live (The Palace, LA, 1995, plus demos)** *Blind / Ball Tongue / Need To / Shoots & Ladders / Lies / Faget / Predictable / Blind / Daddy / Alive / Xmas Song (two versions) / This Town*

**Huntington Beach, California, 1993**
*Blind / Predictable / Broken Soul / Alive / Molested / Lies / Faget*

**Cactus Club, San Jose, December 1994**
*Blind / Ball Tongue / Fake / Divine / Shoots & Ladders / Blind / Lodi Dodi / Faget*

**Dallas, February 1996**
*Blind / Ball Tongue / Need To / Divine / Shoots & Ladders / Lies / Faget*

**San Francisco, October 1996**
*Twist / Blind / Chi / Divine / No Place To Hide / A.D.I.D.A.S. / Low Rider / Shoots & Ladders / No Place To Hide / Divine / Ball Tongue / Ass Itch / Kill You / Faget*

**Kansas City, March 1997**
*Twist / Blind / Chi / Divine / Need To / Good God / Clown / Ball Tongue / A.D.I.D.A.S. / Low Rider / Shoots & Ladders / No Place To Hide / Swallow / Fake / Divine / Wicked* (with Fred Durst) / *Kill You / Faget*

**Worcester, Massachusetts, September 1998** (Family Values tour)
*It's On (intro) / Got The Life / It's On / Twist / Chi / Children Of The Korn / Wicked* (with Ice Cube) / *A.D.I.D.A.S. / Shot Liver medley: Daddy - Shoots & Ladders - Justin - Ball Tongue – Divine - Kill You - B.B.K. / Blind / We Ain't Goin' Out Like That / Clown / Dead Bodies Everywhere / Faget / All In The Family* (with Limp Bizkit)

**Harlem Apollo, New York, November 1999**
*Dead / Falling Away From Me / Trash / 4U / Beg For Me / Make Me Bad / It's Gonna Go Away / Wake Up / Hey Daddy*

Otherwise unavailable individual tracks available from a number of internet sources include *Safety In Numbers* and *Natural Disasters*

## BOOKS AND AUDIO BOOKS

**Korn Bass Anthology**
Warner Brothers 1999

**The Story Of Korn** by Doug Small
Omnibus Press 2000

**Korn: Life In The Pit** by Leah Furman
St Martin's Griffin 2000

**Life Is Peachy** (sheet music)
Warner Brothers 2000

**Issues** (sheet music)
Warner Brothers 2000

**Interview Disc**
CD – Rockview 2000

**Interview Disc**
CD – Megaworld 2000

**Maximum Korn**
CD – Chrome Dreams 1999

**Korn X-Posed the Interview**
CD – Chrome Dreams 2000

## VIDEOS

**Korn: R-U Ready**
VHS/DVD – Eaton Entertainment 2000

**Who Then Now?**: *Blind / Shoots And Ladders / Clown / Faget (previously unreleased)*
VHS – Sony Music Entertainment Inc. 1997

**Family Values '98**: *Blind / All In The Family / Got The Life / A.D.I.D.A.S. / Children Of The Korn / Wicked / Faget*
VHS/DVD – Sony/Columbia 1998

## WEBSITES

For sourcing additional information about Korn, you really can't beat the World Wide Web. There are literally hundreds of sites about Korn containing a wide range of biographical information, pictures, up-to-the-minute news and tour dates as well as MP3's of both their well known and rarer tracks. The following sites are among the most comprehensive and a good place to start finding out about Korn online. Search engines such as Yahoo and Google can uncover many more fan sites. Up-to-date information can also be found on general music sites such as www. rollingstone.com, www.nme.com, www.mtv.com and www.getmusic.com.

www.korn.com
www.thekornkrop.com
www.kornarmy.com
www.kornkids.com
www.kornweb.com
www.homeofkornchildren.com
www.webcyber.com (Josh's Unofficial Korn Web Center)

For details on Orgy and other bands associated with Korn:
www.repriserec.com/elementree/

# PHOTO CREDITS

Reproductions of record/CD artwork courtesy of Epic/Immortal Records

Photos Courtesy of:

All Action London
Pictorial Press London
Redferns London
Famous Pictures London
Rex Features London
Star File Photo
Sophia Reese

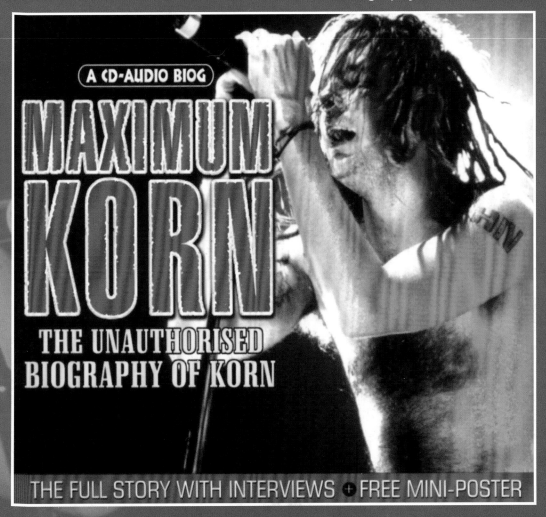